Praise

‖‖‖‖‖ (barcode) T0071887

"Accessible to any and all! The use of concise, direct language as well as the tapestry of human stories woven into the greater narrative make for a truly compelling read. Highly recommend!"
Jude Parakrama Dias | Fellow of the Chartered Certified Accountants, UK

"As much a story of hope and redemption as it is an adventure on the vast oceans of our planet. John De Silva has delivered a beautiful portrait of a life many of us will never have the chance to experience."
Gerard Davey | Musician and Music director/editor, Colombo, Sri Lanka

"This book had me simultaneously cheering, sweating, panicking and ultimately rejoicing. A heartwarming account of a Captain's struggle to defy the odds and finally make it back home to his family. His strong faith in God was his ultimate strength!"
Capt. Harindra Perera | Principal Lecturer, CINEC Maritime Campus, Sri Lanka

"This book will keep you on the edge of your seat until the very last page! As the circumstances continued to grow more and more dire, I couldn't help but clench my hands into fists and wonder, 'Is he ever going to make it home?!.' An honest opening into a man's life, a powerful rumination about a sailor's plight, the value of perseverance, integrity and faith."

Mario De Silva | Chief Officer,
Oldendorff Carriers, Germany

"With such a colorful cast of characters, misadventures and drama it's no wonder that *Captain's Logbook* has received such high praise! A wonderfully entertaining account of one sailor's life."

Bandula Ratnyake | UPS Country Manager,
for Indian Subcontinent, Bangladesh, Sri Lanka & Maldives, Operating from Dubai

"John De Silva has brought the crucible of life-at-sea to the doorstep of all his readers. In this remarkable account of mutiny, monsoons and mischief, De Silva pulls no punches in giving access to the most remote details of his journey, and the harrowing accounts of his near life-ending disasters."

Suresh Wignaraja | Managing Director, Brave
Guard Security Co, Sri Lanka

"An awe-inspiring journey of faith, perseverance, and unrelenting determination!"

Capt. Nirmal Silva | Harbor Master,
Sri Lanka Ports Authority

"Everything that can go wrong, most probably will. That's how I would summarize John De Silva's latest work. An incredible story in its own right,

Captain's Logbook is made that much more powerful as a piece of nonfiction."

Shireen Williams | Hospitality Manager at Guys and St Thomas' NHS Foundation Trust, London, UK

"*Captain's Logbook* was like walking through Dante's Inferno - only instead of parading through hell, De Silva trails the coastal waters of Africa with a misanthropic crew and more cockroaches than have any right to be on a single ship!"

Shawn Johal | Business Growth Coach and author of *The Happy Leader*

"*Captain's Logbook* is, at times, as hilarious as it is horrifying. Amid the baser behavior of human beings, there are acts of true compassion and healing that underline and emphasize the true meaning of De Silva's journey to hell and back."

Rick Orford | Co-Founder & Executive Producer at Travel Addicts Life, and bestselling author of *The Financially Independent Millennial*

"Everyone should read this."

Sanjay Jaybhay | Bestselling author of *Invest and Grow Rich*

"*Captain's Logbook* was a captivating adventure story about the rigors of life at sea and the myriad dangers that accompany long voyages over the vast oceanic deserts."

Samitha Meepe | Master Mariner, Australia

"Nothing short of spellbinding! *Captain's Logbook* has the ingredients of great fictitious narratives, though entirely true, coupled with the granular details that could only come from hard-earned experience and toil. One must-read book!"

Ruki Samarasundera | Freelance Content Writer, Sri Lanka

"John DeSilva takes readers on a dared journey through deep waters... a delightful guide for those of us who want to endure challenges and must-read primer for anyone considering seafaring career. His story is full of hope and sound reasons for faith in God and Divine Providence."

Rasanga Perera | U.S. Military

"An extraordinary account of a Captain's true experience at sea; one that takes us back in time to a completely different era. Clearly written with an easy flow, keeping the reader glued from one episode to another, from mutinous crews to bribery, blackmail and attempted murder. Another powerfully written magnum opus from the author."

Capt. D.J. Amarasuriya | Head of Department, CINEC Maritime Campus, Sri Lanka

Captain's Logbook

Escaping Nine to Five for 24/7

John De Silva

Leaders
Press

ISBN 978-1-63735-056-0 (pbk)
ISBN 978-1-63735-016-4 (e-book)

Print Book Distributed by Simon & Schuster
1230 Avenue of the Americas
New York, NY 10020

Library of Congress Control Number: 2021901581

This book is dedicated to my beloved Dad.

Contents

Contents

Foreword

This was the price I paid for throwing the
word of God under the mat; for the lies, stubbornness, and selfishness. I offer this story to
my creator – the all-powerful God – and very
humbly ask his pardon.
Psalm 49: 20

This is one of my favorite Psalms.

After I decided to quit my job with Green Valley
Shipping and return to the sea; I heard the word of
knowledge during a prayer meeting at St. Peter's
College, Colombo. It was: The Lord says that there
is a person here who is dealing with ships. He has
made a decision. It is not the Lord's decision and
for him to read the scriptures. There was no iota
of doubt. It was a direct message for me.

I was totally confused. Each time I opened the
bible, somehow, I was being directed to Psalm 49.
Therein, my eyes caught-up with verse 20.

On that particular verse, I was touched with
the following words:

1. Has riches,
2. Without understanding,
3. Beasts that perish.

My interpretations of the above were that God directed me to the job with Green Valley Shipping. I held a good position there. I was paid a very good salary, in foreign exchange. I had excellent perks. Such as, free food and accommodation at any of the company-owned hotels. I did a 9-to-5 job. I had a lot of time with my family.

I did not understand all of the above, or maybe I simply refused to understand. All I could think of was getting back into what I wanted to do.

I left Green Valley Shipping, and joined the ship *Cape Agulhas*. The story begins there, the miseries that I had to undergo for a period of about five months.

God, through his message when I was onboard the *Universal Challenger*, guided me to the job with Green Valley Shipping. How it happened, I have explained in Chapter One. God is great; he always gave me the best of everything. It all happened so quickly – one telephone call, one interview – an informal one, I should say. Next thing I knew I was taking the General Manager's position at the company. Very good salary, excellent perks, absolutely no stress on the job.

God knew all the hardships that I was going through at my earlier job at sea. He loved me so much and wanted to help me and my family. He got me a job where I would be able to come home every day, instead of once every three to four months. I was brought back to my family. They needed me. I did not know the value of the job, a job that millions of people in this world would have loved to grab. And for me it was served up on a platter.

Then I suddenly decided to quit the job and return to sea!

Was this really necessary? The truth: definitely not.

I went against God's plan. What happened, thereafter, is the whole story of *Captain's Logbook* .

John De Silva sails on from *Through Deep Waters*, *Sounds of Many Waters* and into *Captain's Logbook*.

John De Silva's story is influenced by true events and captures the suspense, the agony of human relationships, administrative blunders, providence and His guiding presence throughout this testimony story. A book that cannot be laid to rest until the last page is turned.

Chapter One

Turbulence

I was in command of the *Universal Challenger*. Life was dreary onboard this miserable vessel, but I had to endure for the sake of my family–for the sake of my career. I needed to keep the home fires burning in addition to everything else needed to keep my career unmarred. I could not be the one who ran away. What happened to those at the top? What happened to the bigwigs who were immersed in the glamour and goodness of life on shore? They were only a phone call away, but they did not hear our distress calls. In fact, they did not seem to want to hear from us at all–just as long as cash flowed into their coffers, human suffering was of little or no interest to them.

Giving up is not in my vocabulary. Decades of experience at sea made me hold on to the rudder, however shaky it may have been. My contract had to be honored. Whether or not management honored their promises was of little significance to me. Happiness seemed like a tiny island on the horizon, a destination far from reach. In journeying towards that distant horizon, I had to forgo all feelings of warmth, all comforts.

During the latter part of my seafaring years, I never missed my morning and evening prayers whenever I was onboard the ship. During one such meditation, I received a message from God. The message, in my own words, went like this: "When you go home, you will receive a telephone call from a person. For you, this person may not be very important. But it is coming from me. He will offer you a job. Work with him." I pondered this message.

I left the *Universal Challenger* in Singapore on May 12, 2005. After spending two days in Singapore, I arrived home on May 15, 2005.

As a general practice, I typically stay indoors for the first few days after returning home from a ship. The only places I visit are church and the home of my mother. My mood takes time to become lighter and happier as I spend more time with my family.

A few days into my leave, a friend who also deals with ships and has his own business in London offered me a partnership in a start-up business. He was to operate a ship between Singapore, Colombo (Sri Lanka), and Malé (Republic of Maldives) and he suggested that I look after the interest in Sri Lanka. Following the discussion, I told my friend that I needed a few days to make the final decision. He agreed.

Around July 15, 2005, I received a call on my cell phone from the managing director of a shipping company that I had previously worked for. He said, "John, I learned that you were back from a ship. What are your plans now?" I explained the business proposition from my friend. He asked, "Have you decided to take it?" "I have almost decided. He is waiting for my confirmation," I answered. He continued, "Is there any chance that I can put forward a proposal?" "Yes," I replied. He asked when I would be free to meet.

I did not have any problems with him or the company during my command of their ship. I decided to meet with him. In Sri Lanka, the full moon day of a month is a holiday, and on this occasion, full moon day was during the same week.

He spoke to me on a Monday and the full moon day was on Thursday. I called him and, within an hour, we met in his office. After a 90-minute discussion, he agreed to all my proposals which included wages. It was my understanding throughout the discussion that I was to be hired as a consultant.

I wanted my decision to be logical. I felt it was necessary to do an in-depth study of both options. The mystical message I received during my meditation was foremost in my mind. I prayed and decided to take the job with Green Valley Shipping Company. It was an established company and not, as proposed by my friend, a "starter" in Sri Lanka.

I indicated my decision to Mr. Thomas, the managing director of Green Valley Shipping Company, and also to my friend, Mr. Raj Fernando of Universal Shipping Company based in London.

As agreed, I began work on August 1, 2005. I arrived at the office located at Colombo 3 at 8:00 a.m. I found it a bit strange that cleaners were still at their jobs. They appeared petrified when they saw me walk in and it was apparent they did not know who I was. Without disturbing their work, I wished them "Good morning" and took a seat in the lobby.

The next staff member to arrive was Mr. Stanley Fernando, the person in charge of operations and recruitment. Others followed suit and by 9:00 a.m. I presumed all office staff members were in their seats. The Managing Director (MD) walked in at around 9:30 a.m. and sent for me.

During the first briefing, I understood that he had given me the designation of 'General Manager'. The general manager's position is not an 'on call' sort of thing and I realized that I had to go to the office every day. In my mind, I was looking for unfettered work with Green Valley Shipping. During the first "briefing meeting" I made this point clear with the MD and he agreed to my visiting the office as necessary. I left the subject to be taken up at a later date.

My first assignment was to expedite the repairs in the cargo holds, especially on the tank tops and prepare the ship *M.V. Green Valley* for overdue mandatory surveys. The ship was being repaired at the Port of Trincomalee. Prior to this, the ship had been undergoing repairs in Mumbai for approximately one month. To date the company had already spent approximately 70 percent of the value of the ship on repairs, and the consequential losses were a jarring reality. The main cause had been the lack of cooperation from the ship's staff which resulted after a breakdown in communication with the ship's superintendent.

It was necessary to rectify the above situation before proceeding any further. In order to have an overview of the situation, I visited Trincomalee and stayed for one week. When visiting the ship for the first time, I found that there were a few families on board, including that of the Captain. The chief engineer, who was about sixty-two years old at the time, had brought a young girl from Colombo and was keeping her in a motel. Prior to my visit, on Sundays, many members of the crew including the senior officers had been on picnics or spent the day on the beach. It is true that Trincomalee has the most picturesque and 'world famous' beaches.

I also found that a large number of crew were not onboard because they had proceeded home, on shore leave. There were a myriad of administrative blunders. The attending superintendent had been a yes-man to the captain. In short, each and every one onboard was busy with their own affairs and really did not have time to supervise and expedite the ongoing repairs.

After I became involved, the captain wanted to sign off as he had already completed his contract. The chief engineer suddenly became sick and he, too, wanted to go on leave. The chief officer had previously sailed with me and he seemed happy to stay.

We managed to complete the repairs in Trincomalee and thereafter bring the ship to Colombo, dry dock the ship, and complete all overdue periodical surveys. The ship *M.V. Green Valley* was back in trading on October 2, 2005. The MD was very happy. As for me, it was within my normal charge of duty. I had managed to complete the assignment under the most turbulent conditions. I overcame staff blockages and quietly exhaled a sigh of relief.

Thereafter, it was routine work at the office. I began to attend prayer meetings held every Wednesday at 6.30 p.m.at St. Peter's College Hall in Colombo 4. Here I found a large crowd who participated whole-heartedly in prayer and worship. Although I had reservations with regard to the prayer meetings, after seeing a few of my old college mates there and listening to their stories, my attitude changed.

Things began to move smoothly-my job, my family, and my social life were sailing along in unison. I always knew I was not cut out for a 9:00 a.m.-5:00 p.m. office job and for this reason; I planned to leave the company. Soon after, I met a friend who was the managing director of a shipping management company. I telephoned him and he was glad to meet with me.

I met him without delay and explained the purpose of my visit. He called his secretary and requested an application. I filled it out immediately and then submitted copies of my certificates later. My friend, Shaun Gomes, provided me with an indication of my wages and also explained that was the highest wage paid to a master. That made my day! My next sailing job and dates were fixed to suit my availability-late January or early February, 2006.

I knew it would not be an easy task to find a valid reason to quit my job. The MD of Green Valley Shipping Company was not going to let me go so easily. One sleepless night I composed a story–a lie to tell the MD as a reason to quit the job. In the meantime, I prepared my wife. As usual, she asked me, "Are you trying to sail again?" From that point on, she was very unhappy and went on to ask, "Why? Is there something wrong at home or at the office that made you suddenly decide to leave Green Valley-such a comfortable and high paying job- and go back to sea, leaving us all alone here?". A man's tasks in life are not easy. The hardest of them all is to watch unhappiness in the faces of those he loves. The sea, however, teaches one many things- to battle rough weather, enjoy sunny, crisp days, and bask in the quietness of 'nothing' that happens around you. For me, there was much happening in the waves of life.

I was adamant to execute my plan. As soon as I returned to the office the following day, I called the MD and asked what time he planned to be in the office. His question came without a pause, "Is there a problem, John?" I said, "Yes, I need to discuss an important matter with you." He promised to be in soon. My boss walked into the office about an hour after our telephone conversation. I felt awkward about what I was going to tell him because it was not true. I began to practice my story to make it pithy. I saw the MD walking in and after a brief talk with the accountant he came in and sat in front of me with an inquiring look on his face. I knew that every word I uttered would be scrutinized.

I said to him, "Sir, in order to continue my sailing career, I need to keep my sea time in order to revalidate my certificate of competency as Master Mariner Class 1, otherwise I will have to go to Australia for another revalidation course which would cost a fortune. This happened in the past when I didn't sail from 1996 to 2002. I had to go to Sydney, Australia and spend about US$6,000. I cannot afford to spend that kind of money right now. So, I think I will have to leave in order to go back to sea."

It was out at last. The lie had been spoken and I felt much better.

The company owned two ships. My boss paused for a while and said, "John, I am wondering how I can help you in this matter. You know that the wages we pay are much below the standards you are looking at, and with your experience you will not have any problem finding a job at sea with a higher salary."

His statement suggested defeat. He seemed to be giving up and I was happy. But, the question remained, for how long?

My boss treated me well. I held an elevated position in the office. Except for a few days when I worked extremely hard to expedite the ongoing repairs of the ship; it was smooth sailing. Now I was devising a means to leave such a comfortable place where, in my belief, God had sent me to work. I recall the message I received when I was on my last ship.

After I decided to leave Green Valley Shipping Company and take up a job at sea, there was a word of knowledge during a prayer meeting at St. Peter's College. I attended regular prayer meetings held at St. Peter's College hall in Colombo. There is a dedicated team of intercessors who fast and pray for those who attend these meetings. They receive words of knowledge that they then share during the worship session of the meeting. I happened to be one of the persons who received a message. The message was,

"Lord Jesus says there is a person here who is involved in shipping and he has made a decision. The Lord says it is not his decision and for that person to read the scriptures."

The message was loud and clear, and I knew it was for me and I was very worried. However, I treated it as an extraneous assessment and proceeded with my plan.

The meeting with my boss occurred around November 10, 2005, and it was decided I would work until December 31, 2005. My boss went to Singapore with his family during the second week of December. They usually spent Christmas in Singapore. Meanwhile, I carried on with my work in the office. On December 27, 2005, I gave a farewell luncheon to my staff at the Capri Club in Colombo where I was a member. As planned, my last day of work was on December 31, 2005.

However, after that date, I sought to assist the company with a problem on a class survey for one of their ships. Upon successful completion of the work, my boss inquired as to how I wanted to be remunerated for the work. I told him that I did it as a personal favor to him.

On January 20, 2006, Shaun called me with regard to the new job and wanted to see me at his office. During our meeting, he told me, "John, you will be taking over command of the ship *Cape Agulhas*. Be ready to leave the country by January 31." I was elated by the news. Thereafter, I attended to the formalities in the shipping office.

Within my heart, I felt guilt at the prospect of doing something against the will of God and the wishes of my family.

I am one of millions of sailors all over the world. I am a professional seafarer, and I love my job. I love the sea. However, in the order of my great "Love's" in life, it goes as follows:

1. God
2. Family
3. Job and the sea.

My wife admired my seafaring career. I could see her glow of admiration. But there was always a part of her that abhorred the fact that I was a seafarer – for this was a career that kept us apart for long periods of time – long painful days and dark lonely nights punctuated my life and heart. My wife was a director at a company. She was a tireless professional who worked all week and half days on Saturday. Because of this, and even though we planned to on several occasions, she had never been able to sail with me. During the many times I was at sea, she acted as both mom and dad when dealing with family matters, particularly as it concerned our children. At school events, when both parents were invited, my wife attended alone. I knew this was not easy for her.

Each of my family members had been happy when I started working ashore. They probably thought I had put an end to my seafaring career. Now, suddenly, the situation had changed!

We were a close-knit family. Our children could approach us for a discussion on any subject or just for advice. During weekdays, the children were at school and my wife was at work. Most of our discussions were held at the dinner table. We always had dinner together –the family meal. It was during this time we discussed any matters concerning the family. When my seat at the table was vacant, it created a void. And it was going to happen again.

My daughter, who was twelve at the time, asked me," Do you really have to go to sea?" I did not have an answer, and definitely not one that was truthful. As she waited for a response, I told her, "I need to sail to collect the mandatory sea time required to renew my Master's certificate." "I thought you already had that?" she said. She was correct and I had nothing more to say. Then she suddenly asked," Is it because of our very high school fees and other expenses?" "No," I replied, and kept quiet. She knew that her mother was also earning well.

Then it came time for the question from my wife. She asked, "Please tell me, do you have any problem staying at home? I thought you were very happy working for Green Valley. I know your boss is very happy with you. I cannot understand what made you quit such a job. However, I don't want to interfere with your decisions." Here she was referring to my decision to quit Green Valley Shipping. She continued, "My worry is that you will be working for a new company. Although you say that the managing director is your friend, the owners are a different set of people who have authority over the management. Just pray about it!" She paused for a while and said, "I never expected to live alone like this." She likely had more to say, but did not continue.

My son, who was nineteen at the time, did not ask any questions. However, he had this to say, "I understand how hard both of you work. And that is all for the family. There have been many instances, however, when I really needed your help and advice and you weren't there. Especially when it came to selecting colleges and difficult times with my friends, I needed answers or solutions and there was nowhere to turn. If you had been there, you could have solved that for me. And I also hate it when you're absent during school holidays. What is the use of all this money when we can't even go on trips during our holidays? My friends not only visit places in the country but also go abroad for holidays with their parents."

They had every right to ask me these things.

My happiness, I realized, was a selfish emotion if it meant my family was unhappy. My wife and children, especially my daughter, were in no way going to give a nod of approval to my departure. I had already been away from the family on too many special occasions.

I spent that Christmas and New Year with them, but I observed their despair. None seemed to be chipper -- they knew that I was leaving them again.

I will step aside and reminisce on a past event: my beloved father's funeral. I could not attend as I was away on a job. My father knew very well that I wasn't at home. My mother, who had been at his bedside during the final stage of his life, realized one morning that my dad's condition had deteriorated. She informed my brother and asked him to come home immediately. He worked in a hotel about 30 miles from home and arrived in about an hour. As he was walking towards the room where my father lay resting, my Dad told my Mom, "John is coming." The thought brightened his face and he straightened up. The day was April 7, 1989. My Dad passed away on that fateful day. He was just sixty eight years old and God called him home. Whereas, I was in Australia at that time. I am the eldest of three children and I could not attend my Dad's funeral. For us, he was everything.

At times I thought, "Work at sea and collect money." This was mainly to send the children overseas for higher education. My wages at sea were three times the amount I earned ashore. I was not being avaricious but cautious. At least that was what I thought. I also knew it would be difficult to adjust to a regular 9-to-5 job for a variety of reasons.

I left home on January 31, 2006, at around 2000 hours (Sri Lankan time). My flight to Durban from Colombo was via Abu Dhabi and Johannesburg. At the Colombo airport I met the other new-hire. His name was Berty Warna and he was the new third engineer who was joining the same ship. We exchanged a few words and then he seated himself apart from me in the departure lounge.

I was already feeling lonely and sad that I was leaving my family. The flight from Colombo to Abu Dhabi went well. We had a layover in Abu Dhabi prior to our connecting flight to Johannesburg, and we were taken to a hotel. The following morning, Berty and I went back to the airport to catch our connecting flight. The flight from Abu Dhabi to Johannesburg was long but we arrived without any issue.

Upon arrival, and following immigration clearance, we were taken to the domestic airport to board the flight to Durban. There, we struggled with our baggage. Berty, who was in his early sixties at the time, needed help with his heavy baggage. We had to rush up the escalator with our bags; it forms a funny image now but that was what we had to do to make our flight. The flight from Johannesburg to Durban took about one hour and thirty minutes. After a long and tiring travel experience, we arrived at our destination. The ship's local agent met us at the airport and drove us to the harbor where the ship was berthed.

While driving, the agent asked, "Captain, have you been to Durban before?" I said, "Yes. My last visit was about 15 years ago." He said, "Things have changed much since then: once I leave you, if you want to go out again, I suggest you do so only during the day and only with one of us."

A comforting thought. I told him, "There is no requirement for me to go out. I have to take over the command from the outgoing master as the ship is scheduled to sail tomorrow."

We arrived at the ship around noon on February 2, 2006. The second officer who was on duty came down the gangway and welcomed me and the third engineer. It was customary. I went up the gangway with my briefcase and the other bags were brought to the captain's office by two crew members.

All officers and crew onboard were Myanmar nationals. I met with the captain and he welcomed me warmly. I appreciated this very much as I had begun to feel starved for hospitality, warmth, and friendship. The captain was busy with two ship surveyors and he introduced them to me. He then introduced me to the chief officer.

I was tired after traveling for over 36 hours but I needed to start taking over duties from the outgoing master. He seemed very busy working with the two surveyors but we began the transition.

While completing our round of the ship and during our visit to the bridge, I asked him, "Captain, how many generators do you have onboard?" He said "Oh! We have three in the engine room and the deck generator, which is working now." Then I asked him, "What are the conditions of the ship's generators?" He said, "Well, you know, two are under repair and the remaining one is in good working order. The Caterpillar deck generator is also in very good working condition."

I also learned that there was no chief engineer onboard at that time. He had been seriously ill – diagnosed with cerebral malaria – and had been hospitalized at Cape Town en route to Durban.

I accepted the information the captain provided and did not ask any more questions on generators and the power supply. The ship was about nineteen years old and built in Brazil. It appeared to have been built to a special order. The ship had undergone subsequent modification; this was evident from the raised navigating bridge. The ship had three sister ships, all were one year older.

We stopped work around 19:30 hours, and I was physically exhausted. After a refreshing shower, I joined the captain and the chief officer for a drink. We discussed several matters pertaining to the ship and the forthcoming voyage.

The ship was under charter. The captain emphasized the importance of constant contact with the charterers' representative, Captain Dennis Boghart, who operated from London. He also provided an outline of the ports of call for the forthcoming voyage. After being onboard for nearly six months, he had acquired a wealth of experience in the ship's operation and in dealing with port officials of South African and West African ports.

After a few beers, I excused myself, had dinner, and went to sleep.

The captain's accommodation on the ship was very large. It extended from one side of the ship to the other. On the starboard side, there was the captain's office, bedroom and bathroom. On the port side there was the captain's private bar and lounge and a visitors' or family room, dining room and bathroom. During my career, I had seen this kind of construction only in British, Scandinavian, and German-built ships.

I was overjoyed with the accommodation. In fact, I had already planned to bring my wife down during the ship's next port of call at Cape Town or Durban which I thought would be in about six or seven weeks.

Little did I know that this was only a dream.

After a good night's sleep, I woke up at around 0600 hours the following morning. After a hurried shower and a cup of tea, I opened my bag and picked up the picture of Lord Jesus. It was a kind of poster, about 45cm x 30 cm in size. Since the second session of my sailing- from 2004 onwards- I put up a picture of Lord Jesus on the navigating-bridge in every ship that I commanded, prior to commencing my work.

I obtained approval from the captain, as he was still in command, and hung the picture in a conspicuous place on the bridge. The Myanmar crew had erected an altar and placed a statue of Lord Buddha on it. I made sure that the picture of Jesus did not get in the way of their altar. After putting up the picture -- I prayed:

"Lord Jesus, my lord and my God, you are the
Master of this ship and whole universe. I am
only your humble servant. Help me
to command this ship according to your
will and protect the lives of all
onboard-and the ship".

I had completed my first job.

After a quick breakfast, the captain called the chief cook and the acting chief engineer and introduced them to me. He advised the chief cook, "You must remember now that there are two Sri Lankans onboard, you must prepare food not only for the Myanmar crew to eat- it must be palatable to the new master and the third engineer as well." Thereafter, he explained in detail what had happened with the previous chief engineer and that the present chief engineer was here only in an acting capacity as he was actually the second engineer. He also mentioned that management would make the replacement during the next port of call which was Cape Town.

One of the surveyors who had been onboard the previous day returned and resumed his work. In the meantime, we continued with the transition of responsibilities and the captain showed me the ship's bonded store.

The bonded store held all duty-free items, such as whiskey, beer, and cigarettes. One section of the store was filled with various items put onboard by the charterer to use as handouts and for entertainment in all ports of call. Another section held the owner's bond for use by the ship's crew. When comparing the two, I saw that the charterers' quantity was almost three times that of the owner's quantity. No physical inventory was taken: I accepted the figures given by the captain.

I assumed full command of *Cape Agulhas* at 1200 hours on February 3, 2006. My contract was for four months. Contracts usually last for six months but, as I told my friend Shaun, I was willing to pay my return airfare so I could be relieved in four months. That was how it all began.

The agent took Captain Myint Than directly to the airport. Many shipping companies are immersed in cost-cutting measures and nowadays seafarers do not get a chance to stay in a hotel prior to joining a ship or after leaving it.

Crew members may travel two days to join a ship and are frequently seen working onboard shortly after their arrival.

At around 1330 hours, the chief officer informed me that the last few containers were being loaded and the ship would be ready to sail at 1500 hours. I donned my uniform and got ready to attend the departure formalities. It was the month of February so the weather held no surprise. The pilot boarded and the ship sailed immediately. Once the vessel neared the Durban breakwater, the pilot asked, "Captain, are you okay from here?" "Yes. I am good," I replied, and the pilot left the ship. After clearing the breakwater and passing through ships at anchorage, I ordered the main engines put on "full away on passage." The vessel commenced sea passage and increased speed to full sea speed.

The chief officer on the ship also held a Master Mariner's license. I followed the previous master's system and invited the chief officer to the bridge. He passed on my orders to the officers who manned fore and aft stations, during berthing and unberthing of the ship.

He communicated with his native officers in Burmese and I thought it would be best to continue this practice in order to avoid any misunderstanding which could lead to a disaster in our working relationship.

The distance from Durban to Cape Town was 796 nautical miles. Once the ship was well clear of the approach route to Durban, I called the second officer who was the officer on watch and asked him, "Mr. Second Mate are you confident to take over the watch?" "Yes sir, I am confident," he replied. "All yours. Call me at any time if you are in doubt and good watch!" I then left the bridge.

I went to the ship's Global Maritime Distress and Safety System (GMDSS) operation room and sent out departure messages. The most important person on the charterers' side was Captain Boghart. On completion of transmitting the messages, I returned to my cabin. Following my normal practice, I arranged all my clothes, books, and other paraphernalia and went through some of the charterers' files.

It was necessary to study the main points of the charter agreement in-order to comply with them. I was halfway through the files when I stopped what I was doing and took a shower.

Dressed in evening attire, I watched a film while sipping a beer. I did not wait for the film to finish. I had dinner and went up to the bridge. It was around 2230 hours and the third mate was on watch. I had a brief discussion with him, wrote down my night orders, and left the bridge after wishing him "Good Night." It was a peaceful night, except for the noticeable rolling of the ship, and I slept well.

In the morning, I found that the ship had not made good speed even with the support of the Agulhas Current. At the present speed, the estimated time of arrival at Cape Town was 0330 hours on February 6, 2006.

During the voyage, I received a message from the management company informing me that the electrician would be signed off at Cape Town, and his relief was already on his way there. I needed to educate myself on the issue, and I asked the chief officer if he was aware that the electrician was being signed off? He stated he did not have the faintest inkling. I checked with the chief engineer. Surely he would know, because the electrician was in his department! His answer was also "Negative." I explained that there had been a message from Colombo stating that the electrician was being signed off and repatriated and that his relief was on the way. I asked the chief engineer,

"What kind of administration do you run if you do not know when a person from your department is being signed off?" I soon came to find that the chief engineer had two ready-made answers to many of my questions: "I just took over and I do not know," and "I have not been 'handed-over' those duties."

I decided it was too early to class the attitude of both officers as "disdainful." Astounded, I left the matter at that. Nevertheless, I wanted to talk with the electrician. Yet, amidst a multitude of duties, the matter slipped my mind. Important details, such as a lack of anti-malaria tablets — a necessity when the ship is trading in areas where malaria is prevalent - required my full attention.

Chapter Two

Voyage of Rocking and Rolling

The ship arrived at Cape Town at 0630 hours on February 6, 2006. I attended to the arrival formalities upon berthing and went ashore at about 1000 hours a.m. along with the junior third officer. We found the anti-malaria tablets that were required were very expensive in an average drug store. I bought some regardless, however more were needed to meet the World Health Organization's (WHO) requirements. While returning to the ship with my purchases, I met the electrician and another crew member walking towards the city. They stopped and greeted me and the electrician wanted me to pose for a photograph with him. I obliged and we continued on our separate ways.

When I returned to the ship, a stranger came to meet me. He introduced himself as Robert from The Missions to Seafarers. I told him about my problem with regard to the anti-malaria tablets and he immediately volunteered to help. I gave him money and before he left, he asked if there were any problems with the crew? I said that I was somewhat new, and to my knowledge, there were no problems.

I prepared the balance of wages of the electrician and collected his documents; they included a Continuous Discharge Certificate, and a passport. I received a call from Colombo informing me that the return airfare of the electrician also had to be deducted from his final wages. I agreed without further inquiry into the matter.

The new electrician had arrived in the meantime. He handed over all his documents to me.

I called the outgoing electrician and asked him why he was leaving; his records indicated he had been onboard for only three months. He said he did not know why he was being sent back. This puzzled me. For the few days I'd been onboard he appeared to be a good man.

When handing over his documents, I explained that per instructions I received from Colombo, he had to pay for his return air ticket. He reacted with exasperation. I persuaded him to calm down. He apologized and very softly said," Sir, why should I pay for my airfare? When I joined I had to pay fifty percent of my wages in the first month to an agent in Myanmar. How can I go home empty handed?

Besides, I was doing a good job; you can ask the chief engineer!" The poor man was in tears.

I was moved. I could not understand this situation. There seemed to be no rational explanation.

It had been reported that some crew in Southeast Asian countries were charged for their services from the respective shipowner or ship managing company. Besides that, they were also charging the crew that they employed. In countries such as Myanmar and the Philippines, the crew, while working, send regular allotments to their next-of-kin. This was done through the agent.

Returning to the electrician's story, I felt sorry for him. After airfare was deducted from his wages, the balance in his pay sheet showed a sum of approximately USD 280. This was after working for three months.

He did not take the money but took his documents and left my office. Shortly thereafter the local agent called and said, "Captain, I was on my way to the ship to take the outgoing electrician to Immigration, but I saw him and some other crew members in the office of the International Transport Workers' Federation (ITF)." It was situated in close proximity to where the ship was berthed. He added, "It looked like the ITF officer was preparing to board the vessel to meet with you."

It immediately dawned on me that this issue was going to blow up into a gigantic problem. Years of life at sea, scores of seamen, and a multitude of duties meticulously done have honed my senses. I could spot a problem several nautical miles away. As predicted, the ITF officer came onboard at around 1400 hours He asked about the reasons involved in the signing off of the electrician. I explained to him I had only spent four days on the ship and was compelled to act on behalf of the management in Colombo.

I called my friend Shaun, the managing director (MD), immediately. He said he had received complaints from the ship that the electrician was incompetent. He would not employ an incompetent electrician and wanted him gone.

I conveyed this information to the ITF representative. As expected, he asked for documentation to support the cause. I went through all the messages sent to and from the ship during the past three months and did not find a single message pertaining to this matter. I called the chief engineer and chief officer and again asked them if they were aware of any complaint made against the electrician, possibly by the previous chief engineer?

They said they were unaware of any issues. This was very surprising. If the chief engineer was not aware of a complaint, then who was? Under normal circumstances, the master would send a message after conducting inquiries into any complaints. There was much mystery surrounding the dismissal of the electrician.

Every crew member is an essential part of the voyage. It was both a written and unwritten law that no crew member could be removed from their position on the whim and fancy of any one individual, including the master.

I called Colombo again and updated the MD on the situation. He then spoke with the ITF officer and they had a heated exchange. The ITF officer gave the phone back to me and said, "The person in Colombo is talking nonsense. I am sorry, Captain, but until this matter is properly resolved, I have to detain the ship." The case was being treated as an unfair dismissal.

I informed the MD that the ship was being detained and he told me, "You need to call immigration and police and hand over the electrician."

I told him, "In my opinion, he has done nothing wrong nor has he misbehaved. I cannot call the police and complain about an innocent person." Shaun continued in the same vein but he seemed to be talking nonsense. I knew he was going to pay for his arrogance. I advised my friend to ponder the situation and make a decision in the best interest of the company to avoid any consequential losses.

Shaun Gomes, prior to venturing into ship management, was a qualified marine engineer and an experienced seafarer. I never expected him to adopt such a disastrous attitude. The man had changed, possibly due to money, and was trying to use his power now.

An hour later, Shaun called back and asked me to pay the engineer his full wages, without deducting the cost of the airfare. I was happy he had changed his mind. I immediately prepared another wage sheet for the electrician and sent a message to him. Robert came in with the anti-malaria tablets and while handing over the medication said, "Captain, I have to hurry because you are going to have some people coming in." He left, telling me he would see me when I was free.

The ITF officer returned to the ship with a lawyer. He was accompanied by several members of the crew. By that time, I had had enough surprises for the day and asked the lawyer, "What business do you have on this ship?" He said, "Captain, I did not come here to waste your time. I have been engaged by your crew to protect their interests." He showed me a letter signed by all who were present. The letter said it all! The letter endorsed the appointment of the lawyer and claimed overdue wages, reimbursement of leave pay deducted from their wages so far, and the above to be paid and all of them signed off and repatriated as there were only about 12 days remaining on their contract period.

From a seafarer's perspective, the demands of the crew seemed legitimate. A huge wave of discontent hit my very being. I had only been onboard for four days!

I called Colombo and provided them with the latest developments. The MD was dumbfounded. He said he would get in touch with the agent in Yangon, Myanmar, who had engaged the crew.

I called the electrician and told him that his matter was resolved and he could collect his final wages. He said he had to check with the ITF officer. This person's verdict was: "This is considered an unfair removal of a crew member; the owners should pay him at least one month wages in addition to the due balance." I did not refer to the MD on this matter, but paid him the requested amount. The electrician apologized for all the trouble and then left the ship.

Unfair removal of a crew member, arrogance, and non-payment of the crew are sensitive issues and such acts can have a snowball effect.

I was informed by the lawyer and the ITF officer that matters concerning the remaining crew were yet to be resolved and that a detention order on the ship would be served by the High Court of Cape Town. Many of the remaining crew had also sought ITF intervention to resolve their remuneration problems.

In order to get to the bottom of the matter, I decided to speak with the chief officer, usually the confidant of the captain. When I spoke with him he gave a very vague story. He blamed the crew, his own countrymen, for creating a problem. To me, demand for unpaid wages was an appropriate action. An employer should, as agreed, remit the amount regularly to each crew member's next-of-kin.

The cargo work was completed at around 1900 hours and an officer from the High Court in Cape Town boarded the ship and issued a detention order and removed all the certificates of the ship. At 2030 hours the ship was shifted to a non-cargo working berth. Little did I know that this was just the beginning of a long, miserable journey. I then remembered God's message during the prayer meeting and asked for his pardon. It was a bit too late.

I did not get much sleep that night. There were many phone calls from the agent of the Myanmar crew and the previous master. They each spoke with the chief officer and some of the crew to ask them to halt and withdraw their course of action, but their requests did not work.

Now that delays were imminent, I sent many messages informing all interested parties, especially the charterers, so that they could reschedule the voyage. After the cargo operation had been completed, I received a call from the charterers informing me that, under the circumstances, the ship was off-hired from that time.

Considering the worst-case scenario, on the following morning I sat with the chief officer and prepared the wage accounts for the past three months of all Myanmar crew regardless of who went to the ITF or not. I felt that all, including the chief officer, were involved.

The new second engineer had arrived from Sri Lanka to join the vessel. This was great news to me! I was happy to have another of my countrymen onboard the ship.

I was informed by Mr. Wije, the Sri Lankan second engineer, that the crew had met with both the ITF officer and the lawyer in the chief officer's cabin prior to their meeting with me. The chief officer had included his name on the list of those asking for arrears of wages. I suspected that although he appeared to be acting as the Good Samaritan, keen on helping the owners, he was in fact the architect of these events. I did not blame him, however. He also had a family – a wife and two children, and had not been paid for three months. How could the owners expect the families to survive without getting the money from their breadwinners?

Telephone calls continued to come in from both Colombo and Myanmar. The Colombo office informed me they had asked our ship chandler to hand over the required amount of money in US dollars to pay the crew. That was the best news I had all day!

At around 0900 hours on February 7, 2006, the lawyer boarded the ship. I informed him that all of the Myanmar crew would be paid—including leave wages that had previously been deducted. He said that wages had to be paid up to and including that day. I conveyed the message to Colombo and the MD was furious and began to shout. I explained to him, "Shaun, you do not have much of a choice. You have to make the payments or expect further delays and losses to the ship." He reluctantly agreed.

I called the ship chandler and requested him to increase the wage amounts to meet the requirements set forth by the lawyer. The lawyer left my office and spoke with the crew in the officers smoke room.

He returned to my office at around 1100 hours with a few Myanmar crew members and said, "Captain, I have two more points to discuss with you. The first is that I am arranging repatriation of eighteen crew members who want to leave the ship as they have almost completed their contract. The second point is that the crew says you agreed to pay half of my fees."

That was definitely not what I had expected. I told him, "I am the master of this vessel, I did not call you here, and neither did I avail myself of your services. I can only say that you have been a bloody headache to me, so I do not have to pay you for anything." He met my outburst with silence. He then reiterated that eighteen members of the crew would be leaving. I called and informed Colombo of the latest development. The MD was very anxious and said, "John, it will take at least five to six days for me to arrange replacements from Colombo. I have no intention of getting any crew from Myanmar."

I suggested, "Shaun, can I talk to those who want to leave and persuade them to continue for one round voyage back to Cape Town and assure them that they will be paid, signed off and repatriated?"

I heard the sigh of relief from Shaun. "John, please try your best to do something about this matter." I went into my bedroom and prayed to God to help me in this new step I was being pushed to take. I am sure he was watching the mess I was already in.

The concerns of the Myanmar crew were legitimate. One did not have to be a rocket scientist to figure out that they had not been paid for roughly three months. They had kept quiet, possibly because they did not want to create any problems with their previous master— their own countryman. Now that no such bond existed, they had come out with their demands.

At this point, I deviate from the narration to share my observations of the crew. This was the first time I sailed with a large number of Myanmar nationals. We are from two different countries and vastly different cultures. I had been onboard the ship for less than a week. I had unanswered questions, such as the mystery surrounding the former electrician. I could not believe both the chief engineer and chief officer had not been aware of any issues! The chief officer may have been assured of a promotion to master by the former captain, his countryman. But management had other plans. My hiring likely deprived him of an opportunity to get his first command of a ship. This most likely made him very annoyed! The biggest concern, however, was the lack of payment to the crew.

This was a crash course for me. I was confident, with the grace of God, I could handle any situation.

I called the chief officer and asked him to arrange a meeting with all crew members. I told him I wanted it done immediately. He informed me that the crew were waiting for me in the smoke room. When I arrived I saw the lawyer in attendance. I said to him, "I do not want to embarrass you as you belong to a very noble profession. But I request that you kindly leave this room so I can talk with my crew."

Though he left the smoke room, his annoyance was plain to see.

First, I asked if they were ready to listen to me. "Yes," they replied in unison. "You all know today is my fifth day on this ship and the last captain has been onboard for about six months. Perhaps you waited until he left to bring-up this matter, because you did not want to trouble your own countryman and disrupt his rapport with the company. The good news is that I have all the money that you asked for; it will be delivered onboard at any moment. I do not anticipate any problems because the accounts were prepared by the chief officer and I approved the same," I said calmly and confidently.

"Now, the lawyer told me that eighteen of you want to leave the ship today. Who are you?" I asked. Those who wanted to leave the ship identified themselves.

I continued, "Can I ask for a favor? Considering that I have been onboard for less than a week and I am ready to pay all that you have asked, would you consider continuing with me for just one more voyage"?

I had observed that the Myanmar crew had a habit; they always consulted others prior to making a decision. I allowed them to leave the room and have their own discussion. The chief officer and the acting chief engineer were called by the others and they went to join the discussion.

A few minutes later, all who went out returned and the chief engineer said, "I am speaking on behalf of the eighteen crew members. They say that they can give a response only after they receive their money." I replied, "About the money. I am giving them an assurance. It is very simple, if they are not paid the ship cannot sail!"

They went back for another discussion, returned, and said that they all agreed to continue for one more voyage. I asked if there were any other matters which had not yet been addressed. The second officer spoke on behalf of the crew. "Sir, by now you may be aware that our wage scales are very low. We were all aware of the wages we were going to be paid when we signed our work agreements. We did not accept the ITF man's offer to demand ITF wages for all of us since we joined the ship but we would like to request you consider raising our wages for the remaining period of our contracts." I responded," I appreciate your decision not to involve the ITF officer for an increase in your wages. However, I would like to remind you that it's unethical to agree to something and then to demand more just because you have found a deity in the ITF man. Considering your position, I shall ask the company to increase your wages by ten percent from January onwards."

They were happy. I got that for my crew. The meeting was concluded.

I thanked and praised the Lord Jesus. I conveyed the message to the MD. He was very happy and thanked me profusely.

If the ship had had to wait for replacement of the crew, it would have taken six to eight days. The direct loss to the owners would have been around USD 100,000.

When the ship chandler brought the money onboard around 1400 hours, I found there was a shortage of about USD 2,000. I had no option but to cover that with the ship's cash— bringing down the onboard total to about USD 1,500. I paid the entire Myanmar crew with the assistance of the chief officer. They all seemed happy and relieved!

I informed both Colombo and the local agents that the crew had been paid. The agent informed me that as it was after 1400 hours, it would not be possible to get a court order to lift the detention order. However, lawyers on behalf of the owners of the ship were busy working to get the ship cleared.

An hour or so after the crew were paid their wages, the lawyer came onboard with the ITF officer. He demanded USD 2,500 as fifty percent of his fee. I asked for a reason why I should pay him any money. He said that the crew informed him it was an arrangement they had with me.

I declined to pay him, and went on to tell him that I had nothing to do with him and if he remained onboard any longer I would call port security and the police and inform them that he had boarded the vessel without my permission and was threatening me and asking for money. He left my office and the ITF officer thanked me for resolving the problem. I later learned he had charged each crew member an ITF membership fee.

Later in the day, some of the crew led by the junior third officer approached me and asked if I could pay the lawyer USD 2,500 as fifty percent of his charges. "I am not going to pay anything to the lawyer because I did not call him and I did not use his services," I said. The crew left and a little while later the lawyer met with me, wished me a good voyage, and left. His fee of USD 5,000 had been paid by the crew.

When I look at this scenario from a seafarer's perspective, there was nothing done wrong on the part of the crew. They had asked for their legitimate remuneration, which had fallen into arrears. That is their right and nobody can argue or deprive them of that right. My friend, the MD of the company, apparently had tried a few pranks to save USD 600 and ended up losing about USD 30,000— as well as the rapport with the charterers.

Robert from The Missions to Seafarers visited and it was nice to talk with him. There was nothing happening onboard and I went out for lunch with him. Thereafter, I went to a supermarket and bought some CDs and a few other items.

I was elated to be off of the ship. I needed a break after having to deal with so many unexpected problems in such a short span of time.

In the meantime, Mr. Wije told me, "Captain, I do not want to bring you more bad news as you have had enough already, but once we sail......" he paused and went on, "If we sail, I will come and see you to discuss some urgent matters with regard to the ship's engine room."

Soon after I returned to the ship, the agent called and informed me that lawyers acting on behalf of the ship had been successful in lifting the detention order and that it would take about two hours to complete the documentation. I figured that meant the ship could sail before midnight. An officer from the Cape Town High Court boarded the ship at around 1900 hours and handed over all the documents that had been removed from the ship.

At around 2300 hours, the agent handed over the official Port Clearance. I called the pilot and the ship sailed out of Cape Town at around 2345 hours on February 7, 2006.

Chapter Three

The Power of God and Power Failures

When the ship came out of Cape Town, I ordered the engine room to increase speed to sea speed. Thereafter, the ship commenced sea passage at around 0018 hours on February 8, 2006. I sent the usual departure messages and went to sleep. The next port was Walvis Bay in Namibia. The distance from Cape Town to Walvis Bay was about 775 nautical miles.

The following day, I began rearranging all the ship's files and other documents located in my office. I worked continuously until 1700 hours and then stopped for the day. Smooth sailing did not last long; that night around 2030 hours the main engines suddenly stopped. This sudden stoppage was followed by a complete blackout. I picked up a flashlight and ran to the bridge. The blackout had occurred because the only running generator on the ship had stopped due to a cooling problem.

The chief engineer informed me that the cooling water hose had burst and it was necessary to replace it; the time to complete the repair was about fifteen to twenty minutes. Within my short time onboard, I had observed that in any crisis situation, the Myanmar crew had a habit of meeting prior to any action. What they discussed in the darkness, only God would have known. Their meeting seemed to consume so much time and their gathering was not a pleasant sight for me.

However, at around 2115 hours, the chief engineer started the generator and the main engine. The ship resumed sea passage. On the following day there was another stoppage due to a problem in the generator. This time it took longer to rectify the problem, and the total stoppage was about two and half hours. I informed the MD about the stoppages; he refused to hear about the breakdowns. He said, "This ship is the best ship out of the three that we are managing and she ran without any problem for the last eight months." It seemed that since I assumed command all the problems were cropping up. They certainly seemed to be cropping up from all quarters. It was my confidence and the strength within me that kept me going— kept the ship going— and the crew as well. In that moment of time, there was no one willing to acknowledge that.

I did not argue with him. I had a discussion with the engineers and prepared and sent a report to the MD.

I had known Shaun for about fifteen years. He was a marine engineer and we had sailed together. He later worked as the superintendent engineer of the company. As colleagues, we got on very well. Our camaraderie continued while he was the superintendent engineer. He was a very helpful and kind person, always ready for fun and enjoyment. Yes, he was a friend. I was confident in him and came to work for him. I last met him as the superintendent and then after about eight years, came to work for him. The change in him was unbelievable. How had this happened to him? Was it due to money or power, or both? I heard he was very close to a few top politicians. They were also his silent business partners to consider. But the man had definitely changed. I understood this from his very first action; he had wanted me to call the police at Cape Town and hand over the electrician. In my opinion, the man had done nothing wrong, at least since I had assumed command of the ship. How could I make a complaint against an innocent man?

My original estimated time of arrival at Walvis Bay was at 1700 hours on February 10, 2006. Breakdowns while en route delayed our arrival by almost one day. We finally arrived at around 0700 hours on February 11, 2006. I prayed to God that the only running generator, which was also very unreliable, would not stop at the time of maneuvering and berthing when power was critical to avoid any possible collision.

With the grace of God, the ship was berthed alongside the general cargo berth without any problem at around 0930 hours. As soon as berthing was completed, the generator stopped! The cargo operation was completely stalled.

I called the local representative for Caterpillar generators: the engineer from the local office boarded the ship and met with me. I introduced him to the chief engineer; they proceeded to inspect the generator. I waited for the good news that it could be repaired. But my hopes were shattered when the engineer from Caterpillar informed me that the radiator had to be replaced and that type was not available in Walvis Bay. It was necessary to get one from Cape Town which would take a minimum of three working days. I communicated the message to Colombo, and the MD made several negative and discouraging remarks. "Do not delay the ship. Ask the chief engineer to talk to me."

I got the chief engineer to talk to him, and I was sure that the chief engineer gave him the exact position with regard to the Caterpillar generator. Once the conversation was over, the chief engineer told me, "Captain, he is telling me to repair and go ahead!"

In order to commence cargo work I decided to hire a shore generator. That was arranged with the assistance of local agents and a generator was brought alongside and connected at around 1700 hours. I was forced to make this decision alone as management in Colombo was not responding to my calls. Prior to getting the generator I asked both the chief officer and the junior third officer if I could borrow money from them to pay for the generator. That was the dire situation onboard!

The generator was used for two days and eight hours and the rental fee was USD 2,240. I borrowed cash from the two officers and paid the rental fee.

I informed Colombo about the hiring of the generator. There was no response to the message. If I had not made that decision, the harbormaster would have had the ship towed and anchored. If that had happened, the estimated cost to the company would have been around USD 11,000 plus the losses due to off-hire by the charterers.

I kept the charterers' representative informed of all that was happening. I was in a helpless situation and I realized that the Colombo management and my friend the MD were avoiding my calls and messages.

Cargo work was completed at around 1300 hours on February 12, 2006, but the repairs to the ship's generator were not completed until 0200 hours on February 13. The Sri Lankan second engineer, Mr. Wije, advised me not to sail in the night as the performance of the generator remained unreliable. Accepting his advice, sailing was postponed to 0600 hours and we sailed at around 0630 hours without additional problems.

The next port was Namibe, Angola. The actual steaming time from Walvis Bay to Namibe was about nineteen hours. During sea passage, there were about four stoppages due to power failures which caused main engine failures on the ship. The ship arrived at Namibe about thirty hours later than the estimated time of arrival. I informed the charterers of the exact situation onboard because I found that the office in Colombo was playing hide-and-seek with both me and the charterers.

The current situation was not normal in shipping. The charterers were extremely anxious to continue under these conditions!

Dear reader, as you continue, you will discover how much I suffered for ignoring God's message. God loves his creations. That was why he gave me the message. But I ignored him. Now see where I am? The waters of life had turned rough and I was in for a severe lashing.

The attitude and weak responses received from management made me wonder if they were really interested in running this ship.

The ship arrived at Namibe at around 0700 hours on February 17, 2006. The generator stopped intermittently causing power failures, but I managed to complete cargo work and sail out on the same day. The vessel sailed from Namibe at around 1830 hours. The next port was Lobito in Angola and the distance from Namibe to Lobito was about 336 nautical miles.

Soon after sailing, I tried to call my wife and found that the satellite phone was out of order. I called the electrician to repair it, but his attempts were not successful. He confirmed that he was only an electrician and had no knowledge of electronics; the fault appeared to be in an electronic circuit. I was annoyed, and questioned, "How can you have no knowledge about electronic equipment? You are the electrician!" He replied, "Captain, I came here as the electrician and I know only about electrical equipment." That was only part of the bad news. I also found that the electrician was under the influence of liquor. This is the replacement our Colombo office had found for the previous electrician whose departure remained a mystery? I could only imagine the fate in store for us as we pushed forward in our journey.

It was a nice morning on February 20, 2006 at 09 00 hours in the Eastern Atlantic off the coast of West Africa. *Cape Agulhas* was approaching the port of Lobito, and the distance was about twenty nautical miles. The ship suddenly stopped due to another power failure. It was the third power failure experienced during that short voyage. Not so bad, in a way! The engineers got on with repairing the generator.

When the ship stopped twenty miles south of the entrance to the port of Lobito, my thoughts were that the ship would drift northward with the Benguela Current setting in that direction; no need to be alarmed. Further, the current would push the ship towards the harbor entrance. The only consolation during this entire time had been the fine weather.

Aside from mechanical issues, there were also administrative problems. I had not come across a second engineer who was as incompetent as the Sri Lankan second engineer, Mr. Wije, during my entire sea career. If I had to look to him to do a good job and make the ship run then all hopes were lost. He appeared to have vast experience behind him and was also a certificated officer. He was a short man, about five feet in height, dark in complexion, and in his early fifties. Whenever I spoke with him, he talked about experiences he had had on two or three dead ships, ships that he had been onboard which had to be towed. Those were very discouraging stories.

It also appeared that the two Sri Lankan engineers had a negative attitude towards the chief engineer. He was a very soft spoken person, slow in his responses, but positive in approach and trustworthiness. When I pondered the delay at Walvis Bay, it was due to a wrong repair plan and execution of the same. Mr. Wije was responsible because it was his plan, and due to his demeanor, the chief engineer had not wanted to interfere. The end result was that the condition of the already ailing radiator had worsened considerably.

I called the agents at Lobito via the VHF set onboard and informed them that we were having problems with the generator and it was being repaired. As soon as the repairs were completed we would proceed towards the pilot boarding ground of the port. The person I spoke with was Carlos from the ship's local agent at Lobito. He was very helpful and kept in constant contact with the ship.

While waiting for a miracle to take place, I had the worst possible news from Mr. Wije – he had never given good news anyway. At around 1600 hours the generator had completely ceased to function due to overheating. That was the grand finale! The chief engineer came to me a little later and reported that the second engineer had not adhered to his advice. He ran the generator and this action had caused it to cease completely.

Repeating the state of the ship's generators; the three in the engine room were completely disabled and now the only running generator had joined their state of inaction.

I called Carlos immediately and informed him that the ship was now without motive power— it was disabled and required a tug's assistance to tow it to port. I also requested him to advise Captain Boghart. He agreed to both suggestions, and later called and informed me that a port tug with pilot onboard would be arriving to tow the ship. I received this news at around 1700 hours.

Darkness was enveloping the world around us. It seemed so symbolic of what lay ahead in the coming hours. This was a rough battle and those of us who venture out to sea prepare to battle not only nature's storms but also the maelstroms of life. I thought of the divine message— God's message which, in hubris, I had chosen to ignore. I began to pray and ask His forgiveness for ignoring His word.

It was a woeful situation for everyone onboard. Each was wondering what was going to happen. I instructed the chief officer to prepare both anchors in case of an emergency – the ship was in anchoring depths and the depth in that location was about sixty feet.

Suddenly I heard a voice berating another – the language was unprintable. I was on the bridge at that time and I instructed the second to go down and check what was going on. He came back and told me that the second engineer was abusing the chief engineer, blaming him for the damage caused to the generator.

I sent word for the second engineer. When he came up, I told him, "Mr. Wije, I do not think what you are doing is right. We all are caught in a very dangerous and trying situation and we must forget all petty differences and be vigilant. I must also point out that your vocabulary is unacceptable. Please do not disgrace other Sri Lankans onboard by such unbecoming actions." He did not respond and left the bridge immersed in a world of thought.

I was very happy about the way the Myanmar officers and crew acted during this crisis situation. The ship's galley was non-functional as it was an electrically operated facility. But the two cooks and crew set-up a wood-fired stove on deck and brewed tea and prepared the evening meal for all onboard. It was a commendable action. Freshwater had to be drawn manually from a tank which was in the after part of the ship. The boatswain opened the cover of the tank and drew water with buckets for cooking and washing purposes. A few members of my crew supplied fresh water for my bathroom.

It was a great effort under such a hopeless and dangerous situation; the morale of my crew was at peak. I thanked God for their enthusiasm, unity and fellowship in the wake of a calamity. We used emergency lighting after sunset. According to my last terrestrial observation it appeared that the ship was getting closer to land. However, there was no-way to confirm the position. Under the circumstances, I advised all officers and crew members to be extra vigilant.

It was dark in the crew accommodation area and none of the crew members went to their cabins. They were all wandering about on the after deck.

At around 2215 hours a port tug came along to tow the ship. As the tug approached, I called the pilot and requested him to ascertain the position of the ship.

The pilot said, "Captain, according to my position your ship is only 2.5 nautical miles from the nearest partly submerged rocks. In my opinion, according to estimated direction and strength of current, the ship would strand within approximately four hours. Please tell your crew to hurry and give a strong line from the ship to connect-up and start towing." I instructed the chief officer accordingly and the tow line was connected and the tug commenced towing the ship at around 2245 hours.

I thanked God for saving us from yet another irreparable disaster.

Cape Agulhas was a big ship and in a "fully-loaded" condition. It took some time for the tug to gather momentum and pull the ship forward. None of us slept that night. I took short naps on the bunk in a cabin adjacent to the navigation bridge.

At daybreak, we found that the ship was very close to the entrance of the harbor.

The ship was at the harbor entrance at 0630 hours on February 21, 2006. The pilot advised me to drop anchor and release the tug. I declined to do that and said, "Mr. Pilot, you are aware that the ship is without motive power and repairs are definitely beyond the control of the ship's engineers. Therefore, please consider the grave situation the ship is in and take it into port."

Another tug was called and was in attendance at around 1000 hours. The port tug let go of the line and it was picked up by the second tug, which was owned by a private company, hired for berthing the ship. The port tug came alongside and the pilot boarded the ship. As soon as the pilot was onboard the second tug moved aft and was made fast to the stern of the ship.

The tug in front pulled *Cape Agulhas* and acted as the engine to move the ship forward. The aft tug acted as the tiller and brakes. The pilot and the two tug masters did a commendable job and the ship was towed and berthed alongside safely at around 1200 hours. It was nice to be in a safe place.

I thanked and praised the Lord.

But greater agony was yet to come. Everything that happened during the past 30 hours seemed to pale in significance. Local authorities boarded the ship to grant inward clearance. They wanted to take possession of all duty free liquor and cigarettes which were in the ship's bonded store. However, the junior third officer and the steward were smart enough to prevent them from doing so.

Once the ship was granted inward clearance, Carlos came and met with me. I thanked him for his help. I called the chief engineer and the second engineer to discuss with them how we could obtain power from ashore. At the end of the discussion, Carlos left the ship to meet with the chief engineer of the port.

The port's chief engineer had agreed to supply power to the ship and charge for the same but the bad news was that there was a slight difference in the ship's power supply and the port's power supply. It was decided, on the chief engineer's advice, to receive power from the port. Mr. Wije, the second engineer, was given the task of finding a suitable cable and preparing to receive power. After some time, he informed me that the port power connection was at a distance of about sixty meters from the location of the ship's sockets and that there were no cables onboard. Therefore, he said it was necessary to order one.

The second engineer went with Carlos and found the right type of power cable of the required length, as per the second engineer's estimate. I had to approve the purchase order and so they returned to the ship with the supplier. The cable was very costly. Sixty meters of a three phase power cable and the sockets cost approximately USD 6,000. I approved the order; there was no other option. The reefer (refrigerated) containers onboard had already been non-operational for over thirty-six hours and all contained very expensive food items.

Prior to my approval, I called the chief engineer and asked him to recheck if a cable of the required type and length was already onboard so we could save money. He, too, confirmed that there was no cable of the required type.

I called Colombo and explained our near-stranding situation to the MD. He spoke with the second engineer and was informed that the Caterpillar generator had ceased and also needed overhauling. The second engineer said he needed to check the generators in the engine room but was confident that he could repair at least one of them in about three days.

The MD naturally sounded very happy. He told me to go ahead and order the cable; at this time I told him about the cash situation onboard. He said, "Do not worry John, I will get the local agents to pay for the cable." I replied "Fine," and that was the end of the conversation.

The cable was brought onboard.

When the port engineer came to connect the cable, it was found that the port power connection was less than ten meters from the ship. At the same time, the chief engineer informed me he had found a cable of that length onboard.

Obtaining the power supply from the port was more important than a probe into the blunders of the two engineers. The power issue had been resolved. However, we could not supply power to all the reefer containers at one time due to the difference in power supply. I thanked God that the ship's lights were on but it was not possible to run the ship's air conditioner.

The current problems onboard were many — the ship was without motive power; it had been off-hired by the charterers; there were administrative problems between the chief and second engineer; there was no air conditioning or living in the crew accommodation area from 1200 to about 2000 hours; the management was silent about sending any spares; the crew was becoming frustrated; I was under pressure from the charterers to keep them informed about the progress of the repairs and estimated date of completion; only a few dollars remained in the ship's cash; the office in Colombo wanted me to keep them informed of the repair progress; the reefer containers which contained very expensive food items were not supplied with power continuously due to the difference in power supply by the port; the second engineer had ordered a sixty meter power cable and it was of no use now. To top it all, the supplier refused to take the unnecessary power cable back.

At around 0730 hours on February 22, 2006, Mr. Wije came to see me. "Captain, before I go down to start work on the generators, I need to talk with you." I said "Yes, please sit down." He said, "I would like the acting chief engineer out of the engine room so I can get on with my work. When he comes down he starts giving his own instructions in his language and confuses the crew. Therefore, if you and management want the repair work expedited, kindly advise the chief engineer not to interfere."

This was a very serious matter for management to decide. In order to commence repair work, I told him, "Mr. Wije, you are a qualified and experienced marine engineer. I am sure you are aware that a decision of this nature is beyond the master's purview. However, in order not to delay the repairs, I shall advise the chief engineer— subject to the decision of management— to let you take full control of the generator repair."

He appeared happy with this decision and said "Thank you, Captain" and left my office.

After the generator repairs were carried out in Walvis Bay, I had my doubts about Mr. Wije. But I was in no way qualified to endorse his incompetence.

There was no email capability onboard. To add to the chaos, the satellite telephone was out of order and there were no repair facilities in Lobito. Communication was extremely difficult and phone charges in Lobito were exorbitant. A thirty minute call card was USD 50.

I sent a message to Colombo with regard to the second engineer's proposal. I assumed the MD would agree to Mr. Wije taking charge because he had selected him personally. Shaun had also lost faith in the Myanmar crew. An hour or two after sending the message I received a telephone call from Shaun. He told me that since the acting chief engineer and the second engineer had the same qualifications, he would like Mr. Wije to handle the repairs and the chief engineer to keep out of the work area.

I listened to his instructions and requested that he send a message with the same information. Before the end of the day, I received his message and relayed the same to the engineers concerned. Mr. Wije was indeed happy about the decision of the management. When I called the chief engineer to hand over his copy he came up and had a long talk with me.

He said, "Captain, Mr. Shaun Gomes is well aware of the condition of all generators onboard. Please do not think we were sleeping on the matter; we have tried our best with the last chief engineer to repair at least one generator." Then he went down to his cabin and brought back a thick file. He said, "Please go through this— all the messages that we sent and Mr. Gomes's replies are here. Believe me, Captain, unless we receive at least the very important spares, we cannot repair any of these generators. Even shore assistance was previously sought on advice of Mr. Gomes. The repair people who are specialized in MAN generators started work, but due to a dispute with Mr. Gomes stopped the work and left. He is very arrogant; with arrogance and lies no one can get work done." He finally said, "Captain, attempting to repair the generators under the present circumstances is a waste of time and money!"

The chief engineer also doubted Mr. Wije's competency, and supervising the repair work was his best opportunity to check on the second engineer's capabilities.

Mr. Wije had estimated three days to complete repairs on one generator.

Meanwhile, day-to-day activity continued. Except for sending and receiving messages, I had little work. The suffering due to the heat became unbearable. The crew suffered the most as none had fans in their cabins. I had one fan and kept on shifting that to wherever I was within my accommodations. The chief officer had one fan that did not work properly. Cockroaches were multiplying at an astounding rate due to the heat. We could not get rid of them; the aerosol cans we had onboard were useless and the Myanmar crew were Buddhists and did not kill cockroaches.

I did not see Mr. Wije for about five days. I knew he and the other engineers worked long hours. The chief engineer was happily doing paperwork, preparing monthly papers for the company.

It was necessary for me to talk with Mr. Wije as the charterers and management were very anxious to hear about the completion of the repairs. At 0900 hours on the sixth day since repairs had commenced I went down to the engine room. One look and I could see how tired they all were. I went closer to Mr. Wije and asked, "How is the progress?" He said he would like to come and speak with me. "Captain, we need some spares and I have the list." I said, "Okay, you'll need to talk with Mr. Gomes." He agreed, and said that he would see me during the tea break.

When Mr. Wije came to my cabin I called the MD and handed him the phone. After a while the phone was passed to me and the MD said, "John, at present, our engineering superintendent is onboard *Cape Horn* and the ship is in Pointe-Noire, Republic of the Congo. I will transfer him immediately. Please inform the charterers of the present situation."

I had to send a daily message on repair progress to the charterers. I could not lie to them and I told them that due to a lack of spare parts, the repair work was being held up. I told them I had no idea if management would send any spare parts to Lobito but that the company's engineering superintendent would soon be boarding the vessel.

The charterers wanted to offload all the reefer containers but the port did not have a forty ton crane to do so. The average weight of a forty foot reefer container was about thirty-three tons.

Chapter Four

Sam the Man

Sam Neil, the engineering superintendent, arrived onboard at around 1400 hours on March 3, 2006. By that time the ship had been in Lobito for eleven days.

I knew Sam very well because he and I sailed together a few years ago. He met with me as soon as he arrived. The first things he said to me were not very encouraging: "I am not God, and I cannot perform miracles. Just sending me out here is not enough; the necessary spare parts must come! He went on to say, "I am surprised about the careless actions of our MD in a crisis such as this."

I couldn't help but agree with him.

I was very happy about Sam's arrival—for me, he was good company. I received about USD 800 from him for the ship's expenses. That night we went out and had dinner together. Sam was a very good engineer and I had a great deal of faith in him. During the dinner I gave him the anatomy of the situation, and explained the subsequent downward slide into the current state of disrepair. I also explained the administrative problems in the engine room and prepared him for the "politics of engineering."

On March 4, 2006, Sam took control of the repairs and the real work began.

I used part of the money I received from Sam to buy five table fans; one was given to him. There were no fans in the ship's mess and I placed two in the officers' mess and the other two in the crew's mess.

I took a long walk each evening and on this particular night I walked into a restaurant by the beach and had a few beers before returning to the ship. Lobito was quite a safe place. I had walked alone on roads leading both to and from the city during the day and early evening. I did not have any problems with the local people. Many were of a dark complexion and spoke Portuguese.

The grave problem I had in every place was the language. Only a handful of people spoke and understood English. The manager of our agents spoke reasonably good English. Our agents at Lobito were very helpful to me. If not for their cordial and helpful attitudes, I would have had difficulty dealing with the assorted situations.

On the fourth day after Sam took charge of repairs, Mr. Wije came on deck in the evening and asked if I was going ashore. I said that I would love to! That evening I went out with him and it seemed that he was looking forward to a good drink. "Why not!" he exclaimed. "Captain, I am very tired and also frustrated because I could not complete the repairs after so much hard work". I said, "Anyway, you have tried. Do not think about it now — let us go out and have a wonderful evening."

Mr. Wije was looking for a place with music and dancing. I told him I had not seen or been to such a place but we could try finding one. While we were walking towards the city, we saw a quiet restaurant and decided to quench our thirst with a few beers. We got to the place around 2000 hours, and we drank until around 2230 hours. We ordered food — bites as some would call it— to go with drinks. One such dish was fried pork, and when it was served, Mr. Wije wanted an improvement on the dish. He called the waitress and with the greatest difficulty, made it known to her that he wanted to meet with the chef.

While Mr. Wije was talking to her, I observed the perkiness of the waitress. She went and fetched the chef. I saw a continuation of the language problem in trying to explain matters to the chef. After talking for some time, Mr. Wije came to me and said he was going to the kitchen to show the chef how to prepare devilled pork – Sri Lankan style!

The chef went up to a young man who was having a drink with another and spoke with him. I only understood the "Okay, Okay" part of the entire conversation. It appeared permission had been granted for my colleague to proceed with him to the kitchen. After twenty minutes Mr. Wije came out and the waitress followed with two plates of devilled pork that had been prepared by him. Oh, was it good! If only his engineering was as good, I thought.

When the time was around 2330 hours, Mr. Wije asked the waitress, "Do you like dancing?" Clearer than his words, his actions and demonstration indicated to the girl what he meant! She said "Yes." Then he asked, "Would you like to come with us to a disco?" She accepted the invitation. There was another waitress, and Mr. Wije told our waitress to ask her as well. But it seemed our waitress, Maria, was reluctant to ask her colleague to join us.

I asked Mr. Wije "Are you serious about going dancing?" He said, "What else is there to do? Let us go and have a good time."

I was not very comfortable because I had not gone to any of the night spots— the city by night was mostly deserted. I did not want to displease him and appear the wet blanket, however, so I was ready to accompany him wherever he decided to go.

The restaurant closed around midnight, by which time we'd had copious beers. Mr. Wije suddenly asked, "Captain, what shall we do"? I said, "Up to you." He then said, "Let us go back onboard." I was very happy about this decision. Both of us returned to the ship, and I slept without the problems of heat and cockroaches.

Thanks to my companion, it turned out to be a very nice evening. We had laughed and enjoyed the time away from the ship. Mr. Wije, the second engineer, was reported to be incompetent. However, the chief engineer was not prepared to submit a report. I had experienced different situations with the man. I hope to keep the reader apprised of my regard for this officer as well as my attitude towards him. I had had one dinner with the man and it was difficult to rate his competence and attitude from just one evening's observation. So far, Wije seemed okay, except for berating the chief engineer following the breakdown of the only working generator.

On a ship, as at home, we live together. Especially as the master, I have to take action against crew who are incompetent and/or undisciplined, depending on the circumstances. However, considering day-to-day life, until management decided and signed off the person concerned, we had to live with him. In my own experience, when a crew member has proven himself unfit to be onboard, it is necessary to follow normal protocol. Until he is taken off the ship, treat him well. My attitude towards any crew member in general, and in Mr. Wije's case in particular, was based on that principle. I continued to follow it until the last day of his tenure on the ship.

Sam met with me the following morning and said, "Captain, I am not at all happy about how Mr. Wije works. To my understanding, he does not have thorough knowledge and I am surprised to see the things he was doing in the engine room. I am going to revoke Mr. Shaun Gomes's instructions and I am going to call the chief engineer to join the work immediately."

I said to him, "You are the best judge and please do as you wish." He requested that I send a message to Colombo stating— 'Repairs are being carried out but he cannot say how long they would take. The delay was because of the non-availability of spare parts, and that he was picking old parts and shaping them up to turn those around for reuse.' He also asked me to suggest to Shaun Gomes that we place a generator onboard to discharge the cargo and then proceed to the next port which was Pointe-Noire. Shaun had told me many times that he could send all spares to that port, but it wasn't possible to send anything to Lobito.

I was getting to know my friend through the eyes of a ship's manager more and more: his decisions thus far had been poor and his actions were far from exemplary. Disappointing, seemed the appropriate word. I no longer took his plans and decisions seriously.

I sent a message to Stein of Walvis Bay, asking if he could rent the same generator to us for about twenty-one days. Stein responded via local agents that he was agreeable to giving us one generator on lease and the charges had been sent to me; the cost appeared very reasonable. I checked with the agents and was made to understand that they were expecting a ship in about three days and that it would be calling at Walvis Bay prior to Lobito. I immediately made Colombo aware of the generator acquisition, the charges, and the possibility of transporting the same to Lobito. Unfortunately, I was dealing with a nitwit of an MD, and he exclaimed that he was confident Sam could repair one generator and for us to wait until then. When I conveyed to Sam the response received from the MD, he was furious and called Colombo and repeated the whole story. But there are none as blind as those who refuse to see.

Besides being conceited, Shaun was a great pretender and it seemed he had been lying to everyone. It seemed as though we had no one to depend on. However, I had always respected and had confidence in Captain Bogart.

Sam and the crew worked an average of sixteen hours a day. One day, the harbor master came onboard and told me that the port was losing revenue because our ship was occupying a container berth, thus making the berth non operational. He had decided to move the ship to another berth – but not out of the harbor.

After two days our ship was moved to another berth via tugs. All expenses were being charged to the owners account! I began to wonder whether we would receive our wages. I was so frustrated about what was happening that I called Carlos and asked him to check the airfare to Colombo. When I learned the enormous amount I would have to pay, I dropped the idea of leaving the ship at Lobito. I was now facing the consequences of lying and abandoning a good job in Colombo—and also for leaving my family.

The Almighty God knows it all— that was why he tried to prevent me from coming to this ship. God loves us and does not want us to go experience the difficulties and trying times such as I was enduring. And He, looking down upon us, can see all our follies, weaknesses, and temptations. He can see our troubles— and little did I know that he saw all that lay before me.

There was a small church in Lobito. It was a twenty minute walk from the ship. I went there on two Sundays—each day around 1100 hours— and found that it was closed. It surprised me, because I expected the church to be accessible on Sunday mornings. However, on the third Sunday I went somewhat earlier— at around 1030 hours, and found people standing outside; they seemed to have just come out after mass. I hurried towards the church and saw two reverend sisters closing the doors. I ran up to them and requested they give me two minutes to pray.

They allowed me inside and I prayed and asked God to pardon me for my stubbornness, defiant actions, and bad decisions.

Things continued to happen onboard. The good news was that Sam had taken over the repairs; Mr. Wije was no longer part of the generator repair team and I had him doing other work in the engine room. He stopped work at around 1800 hours each day and I had some company on my brief excursions to the shore.

I noticed that slowly but steadily, the Sri Lankans were getting fed up eating Myanmar-style food. It had become customary for Mr. Wije to prepare a dish or two for the Sri Lankans; his preparations were very good. He took over the galley after the chief cook finished his day's work and prepared some Sri Lankan-style curries. I thought perhaps he had been sent by God to look after us in this way. This was another side of Mr. Wije. It was very human for the second engineer, a senior officer, to cook for his compatriots onboard. This was a very rare quality in a seafarer, indeed.

Not only did he create some spicy curries, he would bring my share and serve me in my cabin. I did not like this and advised him to let the steward perform those duties. After all, he was the second engineer, and his work did not involve serving food!

Chapter Five
Repairs and Roaches

Time passed but there seemed to be little headway made in the repair work. Shaun Gomes called from time to time and berated Sam. Once, he screamed at me as well. Considering his position as the MD of the company, I told him very respectfully, "Shaun, I have known you first as a colleague and our relationship evolved into a friendship. When you scream at me, you give me the impression that you think we are on a holiday in Lobito. It makes me very sad. In fact, I checked the airfare to return home from Lobito; I changed my mind as I could not afford the price. Kindly note that is the only reason I am still here. I am praying, Shaun; I am praying to God to pardon me for my stubbornness in making the decision to come here. Therefore, please do not think me and my crew are having a wonderful time here. On the contrary, it is days and nights of misery. We cannot run the ship's air conditioner with the port's power supply, and there are hundreds of thousands of cockroaches on the ship. No one sleeps due to the heat and cockroach menace. Why don't you come and see for yourself? I don't think you will make that mistake because you are well aware of the problems with the generators onboard. Your pretense has put all our lives at risk. I know that you are a very religious man. On every poya (full moon day) you observe Sil (meditation) and what do you think at that time about the poor souls on this ship? That is all from me Shaun. Do you have anything else to say?" He was silent and I asked him, "Are you still there; I know the line is still on?" Then he muttered some words that were barely coherent. I heard them say, "Try to do your best. I will call you again" and he went off the line.

On some days, I started to go out not only in the evening, but in the daytime, too. On many such days, I spent time in the office of the local agent. I almost fell in love with the lady accountant at the agent's office. She was very helpful. Especially when I had to send faxes to Colombo. I found that sending faxes from Lobito was not an easy task. Her name was Nafalda.

In Lobito, all offices and banks were closed during weekends. Therefore, as a practice, I attended to two tasks before banks and shops closed on Friday— I bought a telephone calling card and kept it handy for use during the weekend, and I went to the bank with Carlos and exchanged some dollars into local currency. There was a bank only a few minutes from our agent's office.

On one particular day, I walked up to the bank with Carlos and stood in the line. Carlos stood behind me. I saw a local girl standing in the line ahead of me. She was attractively dressed and not dark in complexion. She was tall and had a very nice figure. She was one of the most beautiful girls I had ever seen. She turned around a few times and suddenly saw Carlos and started talking with him.

It was natural that I became curious; I was very curious to know who she was. I asked Carlos, "Do you know this girl? She is gorgeous." What a small world we live in. Carlos told me that she was his cousin and he would convey the compliment.

As she came away from the counter, Carlos introduced me to her and said, "My captain says that you are very pretty." The smile she gave made her even prettier and she said, "Thank you, Captain." Carlos continued the conversation in Portuguese. He later told me that he gave a brief story about the situation of my ship and the state we were in. Just before she left she said, "Captain, I will pray for you and the crew." "I appreciate that. Thank you," I said to her.

During weekends, if the engineers needed items such as nuts and bolts, wires, etc., Carlos would take me to a place he called the "Black Market Area." It was one complete junk yard. All the stuff found there was used stuff. But the seller had a price for all of his goods. The area was largely populated with shanty houses. The way people here had to live was beyond words. I used to think Angola was a country rich in minerals, oil, and diamonds. What was happening to all the money the country earned? Why was there such stark poverty? It was sad, and sadness met the eye as far as one could see. Carlos went on to explain that the country had an ongoing guerrilla war which ended only a few years ago. It had ruined the country. Thank God the war was over and the people could live in peace and harmony. The government could now use the revenue to develop the country and improve the living conditions of all Angolans.

At around 1100 hours on March 14, 2006, I heard a generator revving and rushed into the engine room. Sam said "Captain, I am trying to run the No. 2 generator which we have been working on all these days." I prayed to God. The generator struggled a bit, started to run, and then settled down to one rhythm. That was good news! Sam told me he wanted to run the generator for about eight hours and if the performance appeared to be satisfactory he would put on load.

While we let the generator run, I invited Sam and the others to go out for a drink. None of the Myanmar officers joined us but we, the four Sri Lankans— Sam, Wije, Berty (the third engineer) and I, went out and had a nice evening. As the engineers were tired, we did not stay ashore for long. After about two hours, we returned to the ship at around 2300 hours.

Sam and I went down to the engine room after breakfast the next morning. After a short while, he put the generator on load, and let it run for one whole day. Once it was confirmed that the ship's heavy lift crane could be operated with the ship's power, I informed the local agents to arrange to discharge all heavy reefer containers.

At around 1000 hours on March 16, 2006, the shore power supply was disconnected. Stevedores came onboard at around 1300 hours and within six hours all containers consigned for Lobito were discharged. Thereafter, a few empty containers were loaded.

The success of the generator repair operation was due to Sam's tenacity. This was good news that came into our uncomfortable lives after a very long time.

I kept Colombo and the charterers informed of the progress of the repairs and of the discharge of containers.

Soon after the cargo work had been completed, the harbormaster met with me to inform me that the ship would be shifted to anchorage. I informed him that the only working generator was not generating enough power for us to start the main engines.

He said "Captain, we have kept your ship in two cargo berths for almost a month, and I am under much pressure from the owners and charterers of other regular ships to Lobito. I have no alternative but to use two tugs and shift your ship to inner anchorage." I agreed to this and at around 0930 hours on March 17, the ship was shifted to the inner anchorage which was a sheltered anchorage within port limits.

In the meantime, our hero Sam continued with repairs to one of the other two non-operational generators in the engine room. The day after the ship was shifted Sam gave me more good news. He said, "Captain, I got another generator working, let us see how much power it will generate!"

At around 0900 hours on March 18, 2006, the second running generator was put on load and found to be working satisfactorily. Sam, along with the chief engineer, had calculated the power requirement to run the main engine along with pumps, purifiers, etc., and also the power required to run deck machinery for mooring purposes. They had come to a conclusion that we had just enough power to run the ship on a short voyage. Far from the requested spare parts, not even a nut and a bolt were supplied by the management.

When I informed the MD about the repairs on the second generator, he told me "John, please do not delay the ship anymore; the *Cape Horn* will be at Pointe-Noire on March 28, and I have already put onboard a hired generator along with many other spares including a radar."

Radar? What on earth?! Shaun Gomes, the famous MD, had suddenly become Santa Claus! There were no problems with the ship's two radars, so why had Shaun suddenly become such a generous person?

I sent a long message to him, explaining the exact issue with the ship's generators and requested he send me a message indicating his understanding along with instructions to proceed to Pointe-Noire.

He tried to limit his instructions to a casual conversation but I insisted they be received in writing, and I finally received his short message. I did not forget to copy the message I sent him to the charterers; I wanted everything on record.

I informed the local agents about our readiness and they wanted to know if I could sail out of anchorage without a pilot. It was not a problem, so I agreed. Thereafter, the local agent Carlos, who did an excellent job for us during our stay at Lobito, came with the local authorities to grant outward clearance to the ship.

Port clearance was handed over to me on March 19, at around 1100 hours, on completion of the outward clearance formalities. I thanked God with all my heart – "Lord, my God, without you nothing would have been possible." I thanked the local agents, the harbormaster, and all others who had helped us during our stay in port, and sailed the ship out of Lobito at last.

After a memorable stay at the port of Lobito, *Cape Agulhas* sailed for the port of Pointe-Noire, Republic of Congo. The distance from Lobito to Pointe-Noire was approximately 469 nautical miles. The Lobito harbor was protected by a sandbar and considered to be one of the best locations for a safe natural harbor on the West African coast. Upon clearing the northern point of the sandbar, our speed was increased, but we maintained a safe speed at all times during the voyage. I had to keep in mind the condition of the two auxiliary engines that were generating power.

My crew endured many hardships during our stay in Lobito. There had been almost no outside communication with families for an entire month. The quality of the food was slowly but steadily declining and the unbearable heat during the afternoons coupled with no air conditioning or fans in the cabins added insult to injury. Yet not a single crew member made a complaint.

One evening as I was leaving the ship, the boatswain, who is the head of the deck crew, came to me with the junior third officer. He had brought the officer to interpret. The third officer very politely told me, "Sir, the boatswain needs to talk to you." I said, "Yes, go ahead." The third officer, speaking on behalf of the boatswain, said, "This person's wife has been very sick. He called her when we were in Walvis Bay. He is anxious to contact home but communication through the local telecom service is extremely difficult, and mobile phone cards are very expensive."

I said "Okay, why didn't he inform the chief officer?" I always wanted my crew to follow certain procedures. I then realized these men were suffering for none of their faults, and the situation onboard could not be considered a normal occupational hazard. I asked them to follow me to my cabin. There, I gave the boatswain the ship's mobile phone and asked him to call his wife.

When the call went through, the officer and I moved away. He spoke for a few minutes and then came to thank me. He said, "My wife is good now." I could see happiness in the man's face, and it made me feel happy, too.

We could not run the ship's air-conditioning system due to the increased load it added to the unreliable generators. While out at sea, however, open port holes provided a welcome consolation. The fresh air felt like a real luxury. But the cockroach menace was out of control. The only solution was to fumigate the accommodations. It was a long process; all crew had to be taken off of the ship for at least twenty-four hours. I knew that under the present circumstances, my friend Shaun Gomes was not going to consider such an operation.

On March 21, at around 0630 hours, the ship arrived at Pointe-Noire harbor and anchored off port. Soon after anchoring, the chief officer reported that the fresh water onboard was contaminated with seawater. Not what I wanted to hear after safely arriving at Pointe-Noire anchorage. Sam immediately carried out an investigation and discovered that Mr. Wije, who was on duty at the time of arrival, had forgotten to change over the ship's desalination plant to the direct supply system, and seawater had seeped into the freshwater tank.

It was another blunder by the second engineer. There seemed to be no end to his follies and irresponsible acts. Sam provided me with a report covering the performance and attitude of the second engineer. I transmitted the same to Colombo. It came directly from the engineering superintendent. He was the sole authority. Therefore, no other inquiry into the matter was necessary.

Shaun Gomes's reply was, "Not possible to make any changes at present. We will remove him on arrival at Cape Town or Durban." What rubbish was this? Another one of Shaun's fairytales!

The ship was at anchor for about two days and was berthed alongside around 0600 hours on March 23, 2006. There were no problems with the generators during the voyage and also at the time of berthing.

The day after berthing, four officers from local Port State Control (PSC) boarded the ship and met with me. I asked the leader of the four, "Why have the four of you come? It is usually only one or two." There was no immediate answer to my question. "We are from four different sections of the port," he replied, after a short, strange pause.

I had planned to go to the local agent's office with Sam to call Colombo, and I was in a hurry. I found that the leader, while inspecting the ship's certificates, was noting some points and others were following him. They were all dark, hefty men, and the leader seemed like a giant.

He suddenly turned to me and asked, "Captain, how is everything in the engine room?" I said, "To my knowledge, everything in the engine room is in order."

Usually, the PSC officers bring their overalls. But none of these men carried these essentials. They were clad in proper office attire. While handing over the ship's certificates to me, he asked for the certificates of all officers and the medical reports of all onboard.

Now, the chief engineer was in acting capacity and he had been issued a temporary chief engineer's certificate. What I had onboard at that time was a faxed copy of said certificate. I had already informed Colombo about this matter but did not receive the original at Lobito as requested. Instead of sending the original certificate, Shaun Gomes had sent another faxed copy in the name of Mr. Wije.

The PSC officer said he wanted to see the full time certificate, and I told him he already had possession of the only certificate that had been given to me. The four men had a discussion and the leader exclaimed, "Captain, I want to talk to you personally." I went to the dining area with him.

"Captain, we have to detain the ship until you produce the original of the chief engineer's license" he said. The ship was sailing under the Panamanian flag, and it is a requirement for all officers to have certificates from the flag state.

I thought a moment before I resumed the discussion, and said to him "Please do not detain the ship. We are already having problems. It will not be possible to receive the original license during our port stay as it would take at least five working days for the courier to deliver the same here."

I had informed the head office many times about the need for the original license and they had both a warning and time to send the document to Pointe-Noire. But that was how Shaun Gomes's system worked.

The PSC officer told me, "Captain, I want to help you but you must remember that I am not alone here. There are three other persons reporting to their heads of departments."

At this point, I interrupted him. "So, what do you suggest that I do?" Then he paused and reluctantly said, "Give us USD 1,500 and I will issue an all clear PSC certificate." I began to perspire. I told him, "Officer, I do not have that kind of money." What I had was only USD 600— that was all.

I am not in favor of offering bribes. In my opinion they were not only illegitimate but unorthodox. But, in keeping with the MD's advice not to delay the ship for any reason or under any circumstance, I reluctantly went against my own principles.

I negotiated with him and finally managed to reduce the amount to USD 1,000. I told him I did not have that much money to offer. After about an hour, he asked, "How much can you give us, because we have to decide soon?" I said that I would give them USD 500. He requested USD 200 more than that amount and I borrowed the additional money from my junior third officer. The certificate was issued immediately and the four men left the ship

I knew that the same problem was going to happen again and again until I received the original document.

It was already 1700 hours and I decided to postpone my visit to the agent's office. That evening I went ashore with Sam. He had been to Pointe-Noire earlier on the *Cape Horn*. He, in fact, had left that ship to come to ours in Lobito. It was a long walk from the ship to the harbor gate. It took nearly thirty minutes to reach the gate from the ship. We got into a taxi, and Sam told the driver where to take us. The taxi stopped in front of a nice restaurant, I paid the driver, and we walked straight into the bar area. There was a girl standing behind the counter of the bar. We took two stools at the counter. We were served locally brewed beer which was very expensive, but tasted very good.

Sam became quite friendly with the girl. On our second round, I offered her a beer, which she gladly accepted. She was included in our next five rounds. She performed a cabaret style dance, sans any scanty clothing. The music was good and she danced well.

Sam told me the night club opened at 2200 hours each day and from that time on the price of beer doubled. We decided to leave prior to that and got into a taxi and returned to port. While sitting in the taxi, I was thinking of the walk back to the ship. As we got out of the taxi, there was a downpour and we immediately took shelter in the security office. After about twenty minutes, a van arrived and entered the gate. The security officer stopped it, and instructed the driver to take us to the ship.

That van was undoubtedly sent by God.

On March 24, 2006, at around 1000 hours, I went to the local agent's office and called management in Colombo. The MD was not in the office at that time and I spoke with the manager of operations. He told me they were planning to remove the crew from Myanmar when the ship called at the port of Cape Town. He also told me that they would be replaced with Sri Lankans. I asked him what action had been taken regarding the present second engineer. He said he had no idea.

Discharging of cargo was completed at around 1430 hours and, as per the port's regulations, the ship was supposed to immediately vacate berth. However, it was necessary for us to remain in berth until the arrival of the *Cape Horn* so they could transfer the generator and other spares from one ship to the other.

The agents were very efficient and extremely helpful. I, along with the agents, met with the harbormaster. He advised me to move the ship approximately fifty meters forward in order to accommodate another ship; our ship could remain in berth thereafter. I thanked God for this turn of events. It seemed like we had won the lottery.

Sam and I went out that evening. We went back to the same restaurant we had patronized the day before. We found that Sara, the barmaid, was in attendance. She served us but spent a greater deal of time talking to and serving an older, white male. We later learned from her that he was a rich Frenchman, a regular visitor to Pointe-Noire, and to the restaurant. The Frenchman watched as Sara spoke with us

It was Friday night and the crowd swelled without a warning. Sara did her best to serve them all and the Frenchman quietly moved his bar stool closer and began to talk to us. He introduced himself as Stefan and we introduced ourselves in kind.

"You know, John; I had a huge motor vehicle tire business here in Pointe-Noire. I used to import tires and sell largely to government offices. I had to bribe each and every person in that particular department to get my paycheck. But, it was not a problem. I learned over time to increase the price threefold when it was a government contract. It was not only a case of bribing individuals, I also had to take the big shots out for meals and they often brought their families or girlfriends. I sometimes had to arrange women for them," said the Frenchman. "They liked white women, so I used to bring down a few young women from France or Madagascar. To be in business, you had to do all that. This girl, Sara, her father, was known to me. He was a big shot in the Highway department. He helped me a great deal and made much money, too. He wanted me to get him a used Peugeot from France. It was not a problem, and I got him one. The man had about three wives. Sara was his daughter from his legal wife," he continued.

After offering us drinks, he went on. "This man, Louis, had been heavily intoxicated once when driving back home after visiting his paramour. Unfortunately, he met with an accident and died on the spot. He had not left savings for the family, and not just one family, but all three! Sara has a brother and two sisters. I helped the family in my own way. This girl was a good student but suddenly became very quirky. She gave up her studies and started working in this restaurant. The owner of this restaurant raped her and she is now in the business of sex work. After work she goes out with rich men." He paused for a few minutes and asked, "You have any idea of taking her out today?"

I said, "Stefan, I am no angel. I might have done that at one time but lately I have started to look at my life differently. So, to answer your question, we have no intention of taking the girl out."

He heaved a sigh of relief and said, "Then I will let her know." He spoke with Sara and then left the restaurant.

I call this a wicked world. Misfortunes for the unfortunate never seemed to come singly, and sometimes tragedy is accompanied by greater tragedies.

Sam and I left the restaurant at 2230 hours and returned to the ship. We went back and talked about Stefan and had a few more drinks before retiring to bed.

On the following day, the sister ship *Cape Horn,* arrived and was berthed behind ours. The agents made arrangements to transfer the generator and boxes containing spares. The ship was berthed at around 1100 hours on March 25, 2006, and the generator and other items were loaded onto our ship within two hours. I decided to make a visit to *Cape Horn* and meet with the captain. Our meeting was a memorable one as the captain relayed his horror stories; he narrated what had been happening on board his ship. Comparatively, the overall condition of his ship was worse than ours. He told me that en route, within about two hours; the ship had taken a big list (inclined to one side). He had instructed the chief officer to investigate and report the cause of the list. The chief officer found a leak in a pipe line leading through tanks at the bottom of the ship causing one tank to fill up and the ship to list to that side. They had pumped out the water and completed temporary repairs to rectify the horrible situation. When the matter was reported to the MD, he had been told "These things happen on ships! You knew very well that you were not taking command of a newly built ship!"

Following many unpleasant happenings, the captain had subsequently fallen ill due to stress and angst and was hospitalized when the ship called at the port of Cape Town.

The captain was a young man. Despite all that had happened, I was sure he had not experienced half of what I had gone through on my ship! I thanked God for keeping me in good health despite the many challenges endured.

Soon after the new generator was connected and the power supply commenced, the ship sailed for Matadi, Democratic Republic of Congo, at around 1830 hours on the same day.

The ship sailed up the Congo River to reach the port of Matadi. It was considered dangerous to enter the river at night so I navigated to a position of about seven miles west of the estuary and the engine was stopped. The ship remained in that position until daybreak. At sunrise, we approached the Pilot Boarding Ground (PBG).

On arrival at the PBG, I had to maneuver the ship for about two hours. The pilot used a small passenger launch to come from the station to the ship and we had to wait until the launch was headed towards the ship. When the pilot boarded, he told me that the launch was the only mode of transport to many natives in that area. The launch was used for many purposes, and it operated only during daylight hours.

Because the port of Matadi was so congested, the ship had to steam up the river for about four hours to the port of Boma. It was necessary for the ship to anchor there but I was dismayed to hear we were expected to stay at anchorage for about seven days. My anger and anxiety were at their highest level; it was not safe to remain in such places mainly due to piracy. In addition, the food situation onboard was shifting from bad to worse. We had had to jettison some of the food, specifically fish and meat. Refrigeration had been sporadic for several days due to power failures onboard the ship.

During the day, the natives came in small boats called sampans. The ship's crew, with my permission, bartered old wire, ropes, and loose pallets from the ship for fruits and beer. Some natives who came in sampans brought live goats and wanted to slaughter them and sell meat to the ship. I did not like the idea. The food situation on the ship was bad but we endured and carried on.

The chief officer requested permission to go ashore in a sampan to purchase telephone cards for whoever needed one. I refused permission because it seemed unsafe to go in the sampans, and more importantly, the ship and crew did not have inward clearance for Congo. Nevertheless, I did not want to displease him and told him I would think of a way to get the telephone cards.

On the third day at anchorage, I called the Boma port on VHF and spoke with the harbormaster. I mentioned the problem with the ship's satellite communication and that the crew were very anxious to contact their homes; I asked if he could help us by sending onboard some telephone cards, and that the crew would pay for the cards plus extra for the boat passage. He immediately obliged; he said he would send a person with telephone cards on the port launch. It was a very kind and cordial gesture on the part of the harbormaster. The launch was alongside the ship within one hour. Several members of the crew and I bought telephone cards and paid in US dollars.

On one Saturday during our stay at Boma anchorage, my mood took a low swing. I felt as though I was battling life from all angles. Not only was I alone in a strange place without the warmth of family, but I was struggling for safe and acceptable standards for my crew. There were so many hurdles, and I could see a greater number on the horizon. I telephoned my wife and told her about the food situation onboard. I said, "I am sure our dogs at home have better food than what my crew and I have onboard at present. Please cook some meals and give them to about five or six beggars or poor people as alms and pray to God to help us out in this situation."

On the following day, I was informed that the pilot would board to take the ship up river to

Matadi. I thanked God, as this seemed like news from heaven.

On April 2, 2006, the pilot boarded at 1000 hours and immediately navigated the ship up river. It was nice to see the ship moving on the river; there were canyons on both sides which provided beautiful scenery. While at anchorage in Boma, I had looked around using binoculars and observed that it was an extremely sad sight. The buildings were ancient. The paint had peeled completely on many of them and they were in a dilapidated state. In short, it was the sort of a place that gave one the feeling no human beings had lived there for many years. The pilot confirmed the suspicion. Whoever the colonial rulers of the bygone era might have been, they seemed to have used up all resources and left behind only a legacy of ruins to the natives.

I hopefully anticipated a better scenario at Matadi, but I found it to be much the same.

The ship arrived at Matadi and was berthed alongside at around 1600 hours on April 2, 2006. When the ship was berthed and moored alongside, I went down to my cabin. I immediately received a call from my junior third officer requesting that I come to the officers' smoke room, the place where we usually met all port officials and other officials involved in arrival and departure formalities.

It is customary on arrival at each port to first obtain quarantine clearance. In some ports, no one was allowed onboard prior to quarantine clearance. However, I found this condition did not prevail in West African ports. When I entered the smoke room I was shocked to see so many people— each one was carrying a big bag. The chief officer, who had been to Matadi three times prior to this call, had already briefed me on the situation. I was prepared to cope with the situation.

I took my seat at the head of the table, and encountered a problem immediately. My third officer, who handled the task of preparing all port papers, had not properly noted the ship's arrival date in Matadi. He had neglected to change the date on the quarantine form from March 27, our arrival in Boma, to April 2, our arrival in Matadi.

The quarantine officer was making a significant fuss about his lapse. I noticed that the West African officials were overly enthusiastic about the smallest of mistakes and rallied around to blow it out of proportion. I was very annoyed with my officer, but couldn't help but think it was my responsibility.

I asked the quarantine officer what he wanted me to do. His quota of handouts, consisting of two bottles of whiskey, two bottles of wine, two cartons of cigarettes and a few cans of beer, was ready. I wondered what "extras" the third officer's lapse would require.

He instructed an assistant to put the "goodies" in a bag and asked to speak with me before issuing the "free pratique" or quarantine clearance certificate. I escorted him to my cabin where he promptly asked for USD 250 to issue the certificate and overlook the fact that my officer had forgotten to put the correct arrival date on the quarantine form. I declined to pay the full amount but offered USD 100, which he accepted immediately. He stuffed the cash in his shirt pocket and left.

Next came an encounter with the immigration officer. According to him, Sam, the engineering superintendent, ought to have a visa to enter Congo because he was not an official crew member of the ship. I argued with him and he said that the ship would be fined for the shortcoming. The usual quota of handouts was given to him, and he demanded four more bottles of whiskey and four more cartons of cigarettes, which I also provided. When all his "goodies" were placed in the bag of one of his assistants, he said, "Captain, I am giving you the immigration clearance. But there is one more condition. You must pay an additional fine of USD 250. We can talk about that later." "Okay," I responded. He then signed and issued shore passes to all onboard, including the superintendent engineer.

By the time I finished with all these officials, it was around 2000 hours on April 2, 2006. I had been on my feet for the past twelve hours and was exhausted. It was my belief that formalities for inward clearance in any country in the world were the same. But, unfortunately, in some countries such as Angola, the Republic of Congo, and other

West African countries, it was very different and very difficult. This was mainly due to the attitude of some of the officials. Matadi had been our worst port of call thus far. Unfortunately, my chief officer said that officials in the port of Douala in Cameroon would likely take the trophy.

Finally, at around 2230 hours, I returned to my cabin and invited Sam for a drink. The second engineer, Mr. Wije, had prepared some Sri Lankan curries to accompany our usual dinner; it was very welcome at that time! We both had a memorable drink and a hearty dinner but it was impossible to sleep because the cockroaches seemed to have taken over. Our sleep seemed to suffer the most, a fact that the management in Colombo did not consider serious enough to warrant action.

The agent's representative, Bob, was a good man and extremely helpful. His family lived in Johannesburg, South Africa and he was the breadwinner in the family. He sent about eighty percent of his meagre salary back to them for their survival. He lived in a room in Matadi and a friend provided him with food. That was his dinner but it was wrapped up with conditions; if he came home late he would not get food because the friend and his family would go to sleep. Unfortunately, he frequently worked late and therefore missed his dinner on many days. On such tired and hungry nights, he would buy bread and have the bread alone in his room with a cup of tea.

On the following day I had to visit the agent's office. As I was leaving the ship, the chief immigration officer came to the gangway. "Captain, I came to see you!" he exclaimed.

I asked him about the fine and he said that his boss would send a letter to me. I signaled to my chief officer, who was watching this morning episode, to give some beer to our "visitor" and send him away. The chief officer was reluctant to comply as he was well acquainted with the "habits" of this officer.

During my meeting at the agent's office, the manager discussed several matters of interest as well as the history of Matadi. The manager was a French national and he was here because of work. He talked about the history of the place; Matadi meant stone, in the local Kikongo language and it was the main sea port of the Democratic Republic of the Congo. It was also the capital of the Kongo Central province. When I told the manager about my provision requirements he said a great deal of the food was imported and was very expensive. This fact was later confirmed when I glanced at the prices sent by a supplier. I realized I did not have money to buy foodstuff for the ship and management in Colombo kept telling me it was very difficult and almost impossible to transfer money to West African ports. I had to believe this explanation for there was nothing else I could do. But the doubt lingered.

I kept praying to God to give me patience and the wisdom to make correct decisions and endure the agonies ahead.

Bob was a daily visitor to the ship on behalf of the agents. He would make at least two visits each day. The last one for the day was typically around 2000 hours. But, on some days, he visited later, too. He was a Christian and a Roman Catholic. I had given him standing instructions that when he arrived in the evening, he could take whatever he wanted from the fridge in my day room. He was very thankful because he was able to make his dinner with the food he took from the ship. I wished that I had been in a better position to help him more; it remains a sad memory.

I observed that Bob was a good-hearted soul who never took advantage of others. He stood out amidst the many parasites we had bumped into. When Bob visited the ship in the evening, he was relaxed and often ready for conversation that drifted away from the ship's business. During one such moment, I told him all about how I came to be on the ship and of my experiences since joining the company. I told him to pray for my crew and I.

God is forgiving, and I was constantly asking for his forgiveness. With God, nothing seemed impossible!

On April 5, 2006, Bob brought a letter from the head of the immigration department at the port informing me that the ship would be fined USD 250 and that an additional USD 50 will be levied as a visa fee for the superintendent engineer. I agreed to pay these fines and said so in reply to the immigration officer. I advised Bob as an agent, to make the payment on behalf of the owners and include the same in their disbursement sheet.

Even after the fine had been paid, the immigration officer would visit the ship every day and demand liquor and cigarettes. Once, he boarded the ship under the influence of liquor at around 2200 hours and tried forcefully to meet with me. My third officer, who was on duty at the time, had thwarted his attempt but the "intruder" had been defiant. After spending some time at the gangway, he ultimately left the ship.

The chief officer informed me in the morning that this officer had arrived with two local girls and sought my permission to bring them onboard. I declined and very clearly told the chief officer that I did not want to see our "visitor." He came to my cabin without the girls. I observed that he stank of stale liquor and wore dirty clothes. He always wore casual clothing though his assistants wore uniforms. This was quite possibly a trick he used to make his rounds without being noticed.

The officer entered my cabin and took a seat opposite me. He said, "Captain, my name is Charles. All the other captains, including some Sri Lankan captains who worked for this company, are my good friends. I used to take them out to nightclubs and I never left them because I should be around to protect them. I brought in two girls. They are not prostitutes. They are nice, young girls and they work for a shipping company. They have passes and that is how they can enter the port. I am off-duty but yet I brought them thinking you might like to go out with us for a drink and lunch. Unfortunately, your chief officer did not allow the girls to come onboard." I interrupted him. "Charles, it was I who instructed the chief officer not to allow them onboard," I said. "Why, Captain? Isn't it customary to meet some good and social girls and go out with them?" he asked in casual surprise. I told him "Charles, you have already put the ship in trouble by imposing a fine. You have been a nuisance at times — coming in here at ungodly hours and asking my officers for drinks and food. I will call my agents and officially inform them of your extraneous visits and behavior which disturbs the peace and normal duties of my officers and crew. You are not a good person to associate with," I concluded.

He pleaded with me not to bring his actions to the notice of his superiors and assured me that he would not board the vessel again, not even at the time of sailing. He left shortly thereafter but not before asking for six cans of beer. I gave him two cans and got rid of him.

Chapter Six

Facts of Life...and Living

This was but one episode in Matadi that I am unlikely to forget. Sensitivity was a lost cause with the immigration officers and subtlety died along with it.

Each time I went to the agent's office, I passed a cathedral which was in a dilapidated state. It was even worse to see that the steps at the entrances and the verandah were being used as a marketplace. The place was very noisy as vendors were busy selling their goods. I learned that it was a Catholic cathedral built in 1914. I went there one day around 1100 hours and walked around the church to see if I could enter this holy place in order to pray. But I found that all the doors were shut.

Bob told me that the doors were opened only during the service. Even though he was a Catholic, it seemed he did not attend any church services. I was not sure if he had entered the church at all. His excuse was his workload. I was aware that he worked seven days a week. Therefore, there may not have been an opportunity for him to attend mass even on a Sunday.

The scene at the Cathedral was a very sad sight. Some parts of it were being used for commercial purposes. Was the priest in charge of the Cathedral powerful enough to chase the vendors away from the church premises? I wondered with anxiety.

We had reached the culmination of a grueling situation and were dying for some relaxation. On the third day in the port of Matadi, April 4th, at around 1900 hours, Sam and I went ashore. Sam had been to Matadi before while on another ship. He was familiar with the town and suggested we go to a nightclub. At the nightclub a security guard told us that it would be open at 2100 hours. We had time to spare and walked to a nearby bar to pass the time. We sat at a small table and ordered two bottles of beer; I was not very comfortable in this place. I found that the atmosphere was not inviting and did not appear safe. We sat there for about an hour, drank our beers, and walked back to the nightclub.

Although Matadi in general appeared to be in ruins, the nightclub was comparable to the nicest nightclubs we had seen in Europe. When we entered, I found that there were more security men than customers. While settling the bill for two bottles of beer, I could not help but notice that it was an expensive place. A small bottle of beer cost about USD 7. However, we sat there and continued to order and drink beer. About an hour after we entered the place, several girls walked in. Among them were a few very fair-skinned women. I wondered how, in this African country, were there girls with white skin? Then I realized that the country had been under French and Belgian rule. More girls began to pour in. Two of the girls came and sat next to us. Both looked very young; one had a very fair complexion and the other was tan.

After a while, the girl with fair skin moved closer to me and asked for a drink. I ignored her for a while and when she repeated her request, I ordered two cans of Coke for them. After that there was peace. Some girls got on the floor and began to dance. It was heartening to see some good dancing. The girls who were seated close to us also joined the others and their dancing left us enthralled.

The girl who asked for drinks returned and began to make conversation. "Are you the Captain of *Cape Agulhas*? Her question almost knocked me off my chair with surprise. "Yes," I said, and was very inquisitive as to how she knew. Unable to restrain my curiosity, I asked her "How do you know?" "This is a small place," she said, with carefree ease. "It does not take time for news to spread," she explained.

This "spreading of news" was certainly not good news to me. A little while later she asked what my plans were. I said that I planned to leave the place in a few minutes. It was quite late. The time was already around 2330 hours. She continued to talk with me. "I am Lisa and my friend is Betty. Yet she is from another town. She has come here to work and fend for her family. She stays at my house." I asked them how old they were, to which she replied, "I am twenty one and my friend is twenty. My father is from Belgium and my mother is African. I have three brothers and two sisters. I am the third in the family. My father lives in Belgium and has taken our two older brothers there. I am here with my mother, two sisters, and one brother. I have to earn money for my entire family and that is why I am here. They wait till I arrive home to get something to eat. We sleep the whole day through and get about in the night". I asked her about her education and there was a long pause. Then she said, "I could not study and qualify and that is why I cannot find a job. Jobs are very difficult. So I come to the nightclub and meet someone and that is how I make money to feed my family. My father left us about seven years ago. Though we wait for him very anxiously – to receive a letter from him or for him to come back to us— we have not heard from him at all. I think my two brothers are very lucky to be with him in Belgium."

I told her, "Lisa, I have a son who is older than you. I want to ask you to stop coming to nightclubs and try to pursue your studies. Get yourself qualified and find prospective employment. As for us, we are not planning to stay out tonight. I am very sad about your life and the situation at home."

When we left the night club around midnight, the girls also walked out with us. Sam and I gave USD 10 to each of them.

They were so happy. Lisa said "Now we are running off to buy bread and something to eat with it." This was the situation— the real story behind the glamour of the girls at these nightclubs. Perhaps it is symbolic of the lives of many of the girls engaged in 'entertainment' activities in nightclubs all over the world.

We came back to the ship and had supper. I could not help but smile; as far as food was concerned, our spread was not very different from that of the girls. It was a nice evening for both of us.

On April 9, 2006, around 0900 hours, the ship was discharging the last container for Matadi. At the moment the last container was discharged, the ship's heavy lift crane gave way. Sam, along with other engineers, inspected the broken crane and found that the electrical motor of the crane was burned out. It was a very serious problem. We could not lower the crane jib and bring it back to rest or to a seagoing position.

At around 1200 hours, the ship completed discharging all cargo for Matadi and was ready to sail. By 1400 hours, the outward clearance formalities had been completed and the pilot boarded the ship. Bob was the last person to leave the ship and he said he would wait at the pier to see us sailing out.

The ship was berthed starboard side to quay. There were two ships berthed very close to ours, one in front and one in back. The ship was ready to sail: the main engines were on standby and the crew were manning their respective stations. One by one, all the mooring ropes were cleared and short engine movements were given to bring the ship out of berth. As movement measures were in progress, the engines suddenly failed. I called the engine room, yet no one answered the telephone. I sent the third officer down to the engine room to report what was going on. The chief engineer finally called and said, "Captain, there is a problem with the main engine. It will take about forty-five minutes to rectify this." I said to him loudly, "Chief, you are talking about forty-five minutes— we will hit the ship behind us in less than ten minutes." Yet it was his stance that nothing could be done.

I informed the pilot of the problem with the main engine. The port anchor was dropped to hold the ship in position almost immediately. The tide was very strong, and the anchor was not holding the ship; we were being pushed back towards the nearest ship. The Myanmar crew did not take any initiative – they were hopelessly ineffective and offered no strength or support in situations of crisis and emergency. Observing this attitude,

I instructed the second officer manning the aft stations to prepare some fenders to minimize the impact in case the stern of our ship came into contact with the bow of the ship behind us. The crew were lacking basic seaman-like qualities and were merely standing and watching the stern of our ship move closer to the ship behind us. I was very happy to see the crew of that ship busy rigging fenders and taking the necessary precautions.

The ship's anchor was dragging under the tide, making redundant the dropping of anchor to hold the ship in position. The ship's backward movement suddenly stopped. At this time, the stern of our ship was only about seven to eight feet from the bow of the ship behind us. The anchor held firm and did not fall back any further. The engine room informed me that the main engine was ready and we were able to maneuver again.

With the first movement, the ship began to move ahead and simultaneously commenced heaving in the anchor. In a few minutes the anchor was heaved in, and the ship moved safely away and well clear of the other ships at berth.

I thanked and praised God for many things: for saving our ship from an accident which would have involved two other ships and for giving me and the pilot courage and confidence. It seemed to come from the outside— a great power, a great strength in moments of crisis— driving me to a point which surprised me. Unshaken, unruffled, and unabated I would pursue—battling all storms, until the skies ahead cleared. It was a strength that surprised me.

The pilot did an excellent job. When I looked at the pier, I saw Bob waving his hands and shouting, "Praise the Lord, praise the Lord." I called him on the hand-held VHF and advised him to pay the pilot an extra USD 300 over his normal fee. The formal letter with regard to the matter was handed over to the pilot himself to be given to our agent at Matadi so that he could receive the money.

This was but another crashing wave that lashed at us. Yet we continued to sail on.

I thanked God for saving all of us onboard.

The ship sailed downriver with the heavy lift crane on hoist position,

The next port of call was Libreville in Gabon. The distance from Matadi to Libreville was about 560 nautical miles. At around 2000 hours on April 9, 2006, the ship cleared the entrance to Congo River and sailed for Libreville, the capital and largest city of Gabon. The port was situated on the Komo River. According to history, the French acquired the land from the Mpongwe tribe in 1839. In 1846, the French navy captured a ship engaged in slave trade and freed all the slaves. Thereafter, in remembrance of the freeing of the slaves, the place had been named Libreville. In French, Libreville means "Freetown."

The ship arrived in the Libreville anchorage at 0600 hours on April 11, 2006, but had to anchor and remain as the port was congested. After anchoring, I went to my cabin to gather the necessary information to send arrival notices to all interested parties. As I was reading old messages, the chief engineer came and asked to speak with me. "Chief, is it very urgent? Do you want some time with me?" "Captain, it is very urgent, but if you are busy, I will see you once you finish your work," he replied. "I need to send the arrival message and it will take about thirty minutes. I will speak to you once I'm done," I said. "Ok," he replied.

I transmitted the arrival messages and returned to my office. I called the chief engineer and he arrived within minutes. After taking a seat in my office, the chief engineer said, "I wanted to see you as soon as the ship came out of the Congo River, but you were very busy during the voyage. I waited until you were free to speak with me."

I said to him, "That is fine, I appreciate that very much. What is the matter? What do you want to talk to me about?" His gaze rested on me for a few seconds. He then said "Captain, do you remember, we had a main engine break down at the time of clearing berth at Matadi?" I said, "Yes."

He continued, "I was at the controls and was maneuvering when I found that the engines were not responding. I told the second engineer to check the air bottles. He went and checked and began to shout obscenities at me. It is true Captain, that I had not checked the bottles prior to starting the engines. I did not check this as it was the responsibility of the duty engineer and the second engineer was the duty engineer. I do not have an ongoing rapport with him, and I did not ask him and I forgot to do so, too. However, Captain, you know that we have the full complement: a second engineer, two third engineers and a fourth engineer. So, with your experience as a senior master, you know that the chief engineer does not even have to do maneuvering. I am sorry to tell you, Captain, this second engineer cannot do "maneuvering," the third engineer does not want to do it, and the others do not have any experience. That was why I had to do it. However, I take the responsibility for the lapse on my part for not supervising my officers properly. But the most important and unacceptable thing happening here was the disdainful act of the second engineer during the hour of emergency. He brought in an iron rod to hit me. Fortunately, the Sri Lankan third engineer, Berty, got hold of him and prevented him from hitting me with the rod. I have reported the matter to the superintendent and he wanted me to talk to you about the matter."

Sam was very busy in the engine room and in the ship's cool rooms. I was surprised, however, that he had not mentioned a word with regard to this matter.

I called the third engineer and questioned him in the presence of the chief engineer. I asked him what happened at the time of departure in Matadi. He told me "Captain, if I did not prevent the malicious act of the second engineer, he would have killed the chief engineer."

I then called Sam. He said, "Captain, I am sorry that I did not talk to you about this matter. But, what is the point? We have already complained to management about the person concerned yet they do not seem to be taking any action. Possibly for two reasons: one is because the second engineer had come only to "help" the MD, as the MD could not find anyone else, and the other reason is that if they have to send him back they cannot charge him for his repatriation, because Mr. Wije had arrived "to do a favor for our MD." I forgot the most important fact: they cannot find another second engineer. Not even from Myanmar, for the simple reason that word has gotten out about our management!"

How correct he was.

But there was no way I would remain dormant in the face of indiscipline. I called in the second engineer and questioned him as to what happened. He said, "Captain, this man has been annoying me for some time and I wanted to finish him!"

That was a dramatic response. A tragedy was not what we were looking for at the end of an already traumatic stay.

"Mr. Wije, do you know that you can be charged for attempted murder?" I asked him quietly. "In the name of discipline, I have to take some action," I said in a definite tone. "Do me a big favor. Please sign me off here, and I will pay for my passage and go," he replied. This was the definition of the cliché "between the devil and the deep blue sea."

I prepared a strongly worded message and sent it to the MD.

I received his reply within a few hours. Arrangements had been made to sign-off the second engineer on arrival at Cape Town. It was a huge joke; we were far, far away from Cape Town. It could easily take another month to get there.

It was remarkable that the Myanmar crew neither took nor contemplated any action against the second engineer for trying to assault their countryman, the chief engineer. If such a situation took place with crew members of another country, there would have been nothing less than mutiny onboard. The situation was precarious. I called the chief engineer and chief officer and let them read both the message I sent to the MD as well as his response. Neither made any comment. Just one question from the chief engineer; when can I go home? He was worried that Mr. Wije would kill him. I instructed the chief officer to put a watchman on the chief engineer's accommodation. He should make frequent rounds and report to the duty officer. I was surprised by his response. He suggested that the chief engineer could engage an engine room crew member to do that work.

I was aghast!

I asked the chief officer, "Is this the way you do things in your country? When you have to safeguard the life of your countryman, instead of taking immediate action, you try to pass on the responsibility? He did not have an answer. I ordered continuous surveillance around the chief engineer's accommodation and noted that he was fully responsible for the consequences.

I had never heard of or dealt with such situations as an officer. I was helpless. As master, I was ineffective. I had not been able to take proper action because management was dogging the issue. A situation such as this could lead to mutiny. It was possible at any given moment! There were twenty Myanmar nationals onboard compared to four Sri Lankans, including the engineering superintendent.

"Lord, my God — when I will be released from this hell?" was my plea to him up above. This trial was what I had to go through and the end seemed nowhere in sight.

Next, I had to look closely at the ship's food situation. The chief cook had cautioned me about the depleting stocks onboard. There were no alternative measures; I had to replenish the provisions. I borrowed USD 1,000 from the chief officer and requested the agents to arrange a boat to come ashore and for a vehicle to assist in getting some provisions. Sam and I went ashore in the boat. Sam was a man for all times and all situations. Once ashore, we were driven to a large supermarket and bought the more important food items. My estimate was that the provisions we purchased would last the twenty-four persons onboard roughly ten days. I planned to take on a big stock of food when the ship called at the port of Douala in Cameroon in ten days.

Chapter Seven

More in Store

During the ship's stay at anchor, the chief officer reported that the crew had discovered a stowaway onboard.

"Oh my goodness," I said to myself, "another problem and a big problem for me!" Reflecting back, from the third day into my command of the ship, there had been a continuous stream of predicaments. With the help of God, I had been able to overcome each one thus far.

In all African ports, as a practice, three hours prior and immediately before departure stowaway checks were carried out according to a specific plan. Yet we now had a stowaway onboard. This was another storm to rage through!

I advised the chief officer to treat the stowaway well. As per international regulations with regard to stowaways, there are certain rules and regulations to comply with once their presence is discovered onboard.

The chief officer had taken the individual to the smoke room of the crew and had given him water to drink followed by fresh fruit juice. Food was provided and he was allowed to rest in the smoke room. The crew was advised not to use the smoke room. If they wished, they were told they could temporarily use the TV room for that purpose. The smoke room was kept locked and two crew members kept a constant watch on the stowaway.

In the meantime, I informed management and the local agents about the presence of a stowaway onboard.

On the following day, the boatswain had taken him to the toilet and allowed him to take a shower. I advised the chief officer that I would like to speak with the stowaway after he had had his breakfast.

Around 0830 hours on April 15, 2006, the chief officer and I met with him. I asked him to sit down. He did not understand English but he did understand my sign language and sat opposite us. I then told the chief officer to photograph him. The language issue was a problem but I managed to obtain vital information such as his name, age, native place, father's name, and mother's name. According to the information obtained, he was eighteen years old. From past experience, I knew that the information shared was not always accurate.

My crew had found with him an empty packet of biscuits and an empty water bottle. It also appeared he had boarded the ship just before it left Matadi on April 9. He had consumed his food and water in the first five days. After that, he had starved for at least a day prior to appearing before any of my crew.

Our stowaway had been hiding in hold No. 2. Once the hatch covers and access port were closed, darkness filled the inside. The hatch covers and access ports were weather tight and it became very warm inside the hold. The area lacked good ventilation.

There appeared to be a fresh wound on his right leg. Presumably, he had fallen from the ladder while descending or attempting to climb in the dark. The wound did not appear to be a serious one but was treated with medication available onboard.

The steward who served him food and the chief officer were the only people allowed to speak with the stowaway. He was allowed to watch TV in the mess room of the crew. He was given clothes to wear, as his clothes were dirty and in tatters, and his old clothes were kept onboard.

After spending some time watching TV, the stowaway requested that the steward let him go when the ship arrived in port. He also told him he had been informed by a person at Matadi that the ship was bound for America, and this was why he had boarded it.

When I saw the stowaway again on April 16, he seemed to be in better condition.

Sam and the other engineers repaired the defective heavy lift crane during the time spent in anchorage. They had to replace a heavy motor and it was a gigantic task.

The ship was berthed at around 1400 hours on April 16, 2006. Port immigration and an officer from a special branch of the police boarded the ship. The stowaway was brought up and the officer from the police spoke with him. Inward clearance formalities were carried out in the meantime. After about thirty minutes, the police officer returned and told me that he would be taking the stowaway. I handed over a copy of my report to him and he told me that the boy would be put in prison until agents arranged for him to be taken to the border where he would be released. He also asked me to provide the stowaway with food, if possible. I gave him some cooked food, biscuits, and also USD 100. The boy was taken away by the police officer.

Each year on April 14, the Sri Lankans celebrate the national New Year. It was around this time that Myanmar also had a significant festival. I felt disheartened and guilty that I could not treat my crew during this season of double festivity. It seemed like all of us onboard had entered an abyss and we were struggling to find our way out. We had a scarcity of food, several technical problems, incidents leading to a mutiny, a cockroach menace, a homemade heat wave due to problems with the ship's air conditioning system, and now the main cool rooms had begun to trouble us after the second engineer had attempted repairs.

Whatever the problems we had onboard, when brought to the notice of management, they fell on deaf ears. The Myanmar crew seemed frustrated as they had already completed their contracts and were unable to sign off and go home. I began to thank God that none of the members of my crew were creating any problems. They had not complained about food or any other shortcomings. This was a tremendous consolation to me.

The second engineer seemed to have "bad hands." Anything he touched broke down. I had to call him without further delay and very politely tell him not to touch the machinery in the cool rooms. Besides the obvious "attitude problem," he was found to be incompetent.

At around 1930 hours on April 17, 2006, the ship completed the discharging of cargo at Libreville, and soon after sailed for Malabo, Equatorial Guinea. Prior to sailing, I received a message from the charterers informing me that the ship had to receive fuel oil and marine gas oil mid sea, en route, from a supply tanker approximately 125 nautical miles south of Malabo. The rendezvous position was provided to me. The charterers also advised that the chief engineer should calculate and take maximum bunkers as the ship would be off-hired on completion of discharge at Douala.

The ship reached the given position around 0900 hours on April 18, 2006. After that, problems seemed to flow like water. The moment one was solved, another appeared as if by witchcraft. The charterers had indicated that they intended supplying approximately 500 metric tons of heavy fuel oil and about 90 metric tons of marine gas oil. But, according to the chief engineer, we could only safely receive about 300 metric tons of heavy fuel oil and about 40 metric tons of marine gas oil. Heavy fuel oil was used in the main engine and the marine gas oil was used for auxiliary engines and for the main engines during maneuvering.

At around 1100 hours, the supply tanker came alongside and the bunkers were received as per the chief engineer's predetermined quantities. The chief engineer told me he could not take responsibility for any overflow or spillage. During the time we received the bunkers, both the ship and tanker were rolling at a right angle to the course of the vessel. Under the circumstances, I had to accept the chief engineer's decision. In situations of this nature, I had the option of getting a second opinion and advice from the second engineer. Unfortunately, the second engineer on this ship was often clueless about both his profession and his duties.

At around 1730 hours, the exchange was completed and the ship resumed its voyage. The next port was Malabo, the capital and largest city of Equatorial Guinea. The country is located on the west coast of Africa and consists of part of the mainland and several small offshore islands. The native language of Equatorial Guinea is Spanish. After a peaceful night of sailing, the ship arrived at Malabo on April 19, 2006, and berthed alongside at around 1200 hours.

The temporary peace enjoyed was lost when I dealt with the officials who boarded the ship to grant inward clearance. As in previous experiences, the procedure in West African ports left much to be desired.

The port's quarantine officer was a female. She was tan in complexion, of medium build, and appeared to be in her early forties. She did not speak fluent English; the local agent, who was also a female, had to do a great deal of interpretation.

Once the quarantine officer's work was over, she was given her quota of handouts which included three bottles of white wine, three bottles of red wine, two cartons of cigarettes and some food stuff. After receiving her handouts, we expected her to leave, but she did not. Other individuals began to walk in, including a hefty man, the chief customs officer, and his team, as well as immigration officers and others.

The chief customs officer did not join me at the table but made himself comfortable on a couch and asked for a bottle of whiskey for himself and two of his friends. The bottle was opened right there and they began to party. He requested sodas and some 'bites;' I got him what he wanted, and made sure he was comfortable. From time to time I watched them and wondered how on earth these people drank whiskey as it was very warm inside the ship. Without air conditioning we were perspiring from every part of our bodies. A little while later came another request— he wanted lunch onboard; this was also arranged. They finished the bottle of whiskey, had lunch, collected their quota of handouts, and then left the ship. The customs officers, immigration officers, and their companions left the ship as well.

The only person who remained was the lady who first boarded the ship, the quarantine officer. She had finished a few cans of Coke and had told the agent that she wanted to come to my cabin and talk with me. I wondered what the essence of this secret conversation could be. I could almost hear the chuckles of my third officer and the steward, who were always with me until all formalities had been completed. At this moment, however, they could not leave as there was still a formality onboard.

"Yes, Madame, what can I do for you?" I asked her. "Go to your cabin," she urged with a smile. At this point, the agent told me she had to get back to the office to prepare the departure papers as the ship's stay in that port was only about four hours. The chief officer arrived and told me that there was a problem and that the stevedores were asking our crew to unleash the containers. This was usually done by the stevedores. "Let the stevedores do it," I told him.

A little while later, another person arrived and introduced himself as a representative of the charterers. He wanted me to instruct the crew to unleash the cargo. He seemed arrogant and his attitude spurred me to decline.

During this commotion, the lady quarantine officer, too, had left.

It was time for me to send the arrival report and I went into the GMDSS room to do so. On opening email, I saw that there was a message from the charterers. They had requested that I engage the ship's crew to unleash the containers; this was to avoid any delay in sailing. The reason given was that the port was short of labor and there were an inadequate number of workers to complete the task.

There wasn't any cargo to load. If the ship did not complete cargo operation and sail before sunset, sailing would have to be postponed until the following day. I was aware that the charterers had already planned to discharge the balance of the cargo at Douala and off- hire the ship without further delay.

I instructed the chief officer to unlash and prepare the containers for discharge. He left my cabin to instruct the ship's crew. A little while later, the chief officer returned and said, "Captain, the crew is on the job but they have a request." "What is it?" I asked with rising curiosity. Then he said, "The crew is asking for payment for the extra work. I communicated the request to the charterers and received a reply offering USD 250. I agreed and thanked them for the offer. All containers for Malabo were discharged and the ship sailed at 1730 hours for the port of Douala.

My crew, especially the chief officer, reiterated to me that the customs officers who boarded to grant inward clearance at the port of Douala had a habit of taking everything in the ship's bonded store. The PSC officer was an additional problem. I had a discussion with the chief officer and third officer in an effort to prepare for these possible looters. Following our discussion, it was decided to separate the handout quota of each boarding party. For example, bottles of whiskey, cartons of cigarettes, and wine for the port quarantine, immigration, and other officers. A few cases of beer, a few bottles of whiskey, and several bottles of wine, along with a few cartons of cigarettes, were set aside for customs to take. Once this segregation was carried out, whatever remained was to be immediately removed and given to officers and crew for safekeeping.

I received a message from the charterers during the voyage to Douala which asked me to prepare all material onboard which belonged to them to discharge ashore at Douala; especially the spare reefer containers. These were obviously very expensive items. In the same message, it was mentioned that the charterers' bonus paid to crew on completion of each voyage would be paid at Douala. It was also mentioned that they were unable to pay the $1,500 in US dollars, due to foreign exchange regulations in Cameroon, and had requested me to accept the same in Cameroon francs. The same message applied to the container unlashing allowance at Malabo.

I discussed the matter with the chief officer: I suggested that as we were not receiving any ship's food allowance for the ship's officers and crew from the company, I would use the money for that purpose and then have the company reimburse the same at Cape Town. He was happy and readily agreed to my proposition. After my discussion with the chief officer, I informed the charterers that the crew agreed to their offer.

All officials, except customs, boarded the ship and completed their part of the formalities. I finished work for the day around 0300 hours and went to bed. I was up by 0600 hours the next morning, which was typical for me, regardless of the time I go to sleep each day

At around 0730 hours, the junior third officer called and informed me that the customs officers were onboard. I went down and found that there were three of them, two males and a nice-looking young female.

The junior third officer brought in the papers which were scrutinized by them all. I found that their eyes were well-focused on the bonded stores' list. "Captain, you have a very small quantity in the bonded stores," one of them remarked. I said to him, "Officer that is all we have onboard." Thereafter, the three of them got into a very serious discussion in their language. Suddenly, one of the male officers said that they wanted to see our bonded stores. "Most certainly," I said, and instructed the junior third officer to go with them and show them the inventory in the store. As they were leaving, I said to them, "The three of you may take everything that is in the stores, and share it among yourselves." Their faces lit up with bright smiles. They returned with their loot. The most shocking scene was to see the lady officer carrying two cases of beer, and my junior third officer following them empty-handed. I reprimanded him for not helping the lady. "No sir, I offered to help her but she would not let me carry anything," he replied. The lady officer confirmed what was being said.

I could not help but observe how lethargic my Myanmar steward was. He was serving them cold drinks. I instructed him to serve them tea or coffee and they warmed towards the idea. A sense of happiness and content prevailed and they began to talk with me until the hot drinks were served. One of the men asked, "Captain, have you been to Douala before?" "No, this is the first time," I said. "Do you know that there are some good nightclubs in the city, where you can listen to good music, dance, and have a good time?" "How can I dance alone? I must have a partner," I lamented. "Oh, when you go there you will find many, many girls," he consoled.

The lady officer was listening to our conversation, laughing, and enjoying the banter.

I turned around and asked her, "Would you like to join me to go to a nightclub one evening?" "Yes, she is not married, she can join you," both the males suggested. She asked me when I would like to go. "Let me finish with the ship's work and I will let you know," I told her.

"Captain, you have got to be careful at night because the place is not safe," warned one of the male officers. I thanked him for the advice. Once the coffee was served, they enjoyed it and left the ship.

The ship, whether at sea or in port, was always swinging with action. However, not all action was pleasant. A few minutes after the customs officers had gone, the ship's agent boarded and met with me. He said that his manager wanted to see me because there was a problem with the money that the agent had to pay the ship on behalf of the charterers. I accompanied him to the agent's office and met with the manager. He was a South African national. "I am here because you wanted to see me about a problem with regard to the money that is owed to me," I told him. "Captain, please sit down. There was no problem at all with the money that we have to pay you. Our chief accountant will explain everything to you." He accompanied me to the office of the chief accountant and introduced me. The chief accountant was an Indian national.

"Captain, the cash is ready. But we did not want to hand it over to our man, Lewis, because we do not trust him," he explained.

This seemed to be an uncertain situation, where even a colleague could not be trusted. Trust, in my mind, was an essential factor. My whole life, work, and emotions rested on trust. Yet here, there was little or no trust in the air. How unhappy and unsure they must all be.

"They are good people but with money, especially a lot of money, we just cannot trust them. There is a good possibility that he would take a bundle or two and say that was all I gave him. Because, as you can see USD 1,750, is a lot of money in Cameroon francs. You know francs have no value at all," he explained.

More negativity, I thought. First, distrust and now disdain and disgust. The currency conversion, as I remember, was one US dollar to about 480 Cameroon francs. I then realized the need for this whole exercise. I collected a big bag of money and left the office with Lewis.

When I returned to the ship, the chief officer gave me the good news that the PSC officer had boarded the ship during my absence. The chief officer had dealt with him and as I was not onboard. He had looked at the PSC certificate issued at Pointe-Noire, and had left the ship with his quota of handouts. This news brought me great relief.

Two ship chandlers met with me, submitted quotations, and offered their services. I selected one and handed over the provisions order to him. I found that every item of food was very expensive. I was forced to reduce the quantity of several items.

In the meantime, the chief engineer informed me that there was a man onboard to buy sludge and sought my permission to discharge the sludge ashore. I granted permission and said that I needed a part of that money to pay for provisions. He agreed and went away. It is customary on some ships that part of the monies earned by way of disposing sludge and other waste is taken by the chief engineer. The balance can be distributed among other engineers and engine room ratings. Much depended on the chief engineer; some of them extended the benefit to cooks, stewards, and deck crew as well.

I bought six table fans and two pedestal fans for the ship from the money I received for the sludge. Part of the money was also spent on buying Freon gas to restart the ship's air conditioning system, and for the domestic cool rooms. I was happy I was able to accumulate some money, though not by the most sophisticated means, to handle the ship's immediate expenses. Managing the ship's finances was a task that weighed me down immensely.

With everything falling into place, the last task to be handled was bad news. But that is how the waters of life flow; unexpected boulders arise and darkened skies take over blue-hued hopes.

The MD sent a message instructing me to arrange to sign off Sam and repatriate him to

Colombo. I called the agents and conveyed to them the message I had received from Colombo. I received a response from them in about two hours: the agents advised me to sign off Sam and informed me that repatriation had been arranged.

For Sam, however, the news was heartening. I knew I was going to miss him. He was great company and I had discussed several matters pertaining to the ship and its operations with him. But it was natural that Sam was overjoyed with the news that he was going back home.

I dreamed about my departure. In my prayers, I asked God, "When will my day come?"

On hearing the news that the engineering superintendent was being signed off and repatriated, some of my crew members were excited and wanted to know why he could leave Douala and they could not. When they came to me, I said, "The charterers could not pay your allowance of USD 1,750 due to the prevailing foreign exchange regulations in Cameroon. How do you expect management to pay salaries of two months in US dollars?"

They never discussed the subject with me again. Dealing with members of the crew always required a certain degree of skill and tact. And with the crew from Myanmar, one had to be more than articulate. It was necessary to be observant, shrewd, and farsighted to overcome impending disasters. The crew, based on past records, were both silent and dangerous.

On April 23, 2006, I received another message from the charterers confirming that the ship would be off-hired on completion of the discharge of cargo at Douala. Although it was not news to me, I was very sad because they were good charterers. I had a satisfactory rapport with them, particularly with Captain Boghart. I could not forget the fact that the charterers had helped me on innumerable occasions when we were in trouble.

I went out to dinner with Sam that evening. It was an act of camaraderie. He was expected to leave on April 24. We went to a Chinese restaurant and had several beers before we ordered dinner. Although we wanted to go to a nightclub, we changed our minds as we did not have the money. We returned to the ship and slept with the cockroaches.

On April 24, the agent informed me that he would be arriving at around 2000 hours to take Sam to the airport. On that day, at around 1900 hours, Sam was ready to leave. He was in my cabin having a beer when a person in a white uniform stormed into my day room and exclaimed, "Captain, you are sitting here. Don't you know what is happening outside? I have already informed the harbormaster with regard to what I have observed. Come with me!" he urged. Sam and I followed him to the deck on the after part of the ship. As my eyes rested upon the object of dissent, I was both startled and shocked. There were about eight cans filled with marine gas oil. I summoned the duty officer and the watchman on gangway duty. They said that they had not seen the cans before and, to their knowledge, nothing had left the ship.

It was a lie! The officer pointed out some men hiding on the side of a warehouse; according to him, they had been buying oil from the ship.

The chief officer and chief engineer were not onboard. Sam called the duty engineer, the fourth engineer who was also a Myanmar national, and questioned him as to how these large cans (each about twenty liters) were filled with gas oil and brought on deck. He said he was not aware of anything untoward happening. The engineering cadet who was on duty in the engine room was called. After an initial interrogation, I almost threatened him. The young apprentice was shaken and blurted out that he had filled the cans and brought them up to replenish the oil tank of the deck generator. On further questioning, he confessed and said that he wanted to sell the oil and had brought the cans up and kept them on the deck. When I asked him whether he had already sold any oil, he said, "No."

This denial, however, was hard to believe.

My biggest problem and worry right now was this man from the port. While Sam was continuing with the inquiry, I called the officer from the port and pleaded with him not to take any action because it was confirmed that no oil had been sold. After a great deal of bragging, he said, "OK,

Captain, tomorrow is my day off but I will come in the morning and I do not want to waste any time on the ship. For the favor I did for the ship, I want you to give me a "good present." Therefore, please see that you have that ready by 10:00 tomorrow morning." He left thereafter.

I called the engineering cadet and explained the situation to him, he agreed to pay the port officer. Sam and I discussed the matter, and our conclusion was that this was not a plan of the young apprentice. The senior engineer and the other crew of the engine room had to be involved. But the young man's loyalty to his superiors ironically made him disloyal to his employer. He went further and told me that he was ready to face any punishment.

It seemed that the intrigue had been well-planned; the senior engineers including the Sri Lankan second engineer had disappeared from the scene. This was a case of infraction of all company rules and regulations. It was a grueling situation for me, as I was responsible for all happenings onboard. I was responsible not only for the crew but for the fruits of their actions—however fresh or rotten they might be.

Sam left the ship that night. His departure was a huge blow to me.

On the following day, at around 1000 hours, the officer came onboard. I called the chief engineer and the second engineer and told them that it was their responsibility to decide how the payment would be made. The apprentice's monthly allowance was only USD 150. Therefore that amount was paid to the port's officer as "a bribe." He left with the money.

I sent a detailed report to Colombo, but I wonder if anybody read it.

Considering what happened with the reports I had sent in the past, I knew it was a waste of time, but putting it on record was very important. All the materials onboard which belonged to the charterers were discharged ashore. They thanked me profusely on receipt as all the items were discharged as per the inventory.

On April 26, the discharging of cargo was completed at 0200 hours, and the ship was off-hired. The ship was shifted to outer anchorage on the instructions of the owners.

After a few days at anchorage, we were once again facing a food shortage. I sought the assistance of the charterers and was informed that as the ship was anchored about eight nautical miles away from the port, I would be required to spend about USD 800 just to hire a boat to transport provisions. I did not have that much money.

Chapter Eight

Borrowing, Supplying, and Sailing

G od was great. A few days later, on May 7, 2006, I was informed by the owners that the surveyor would be arriving on board to carry out a comprehensive survey of the ship; he would also be staying onboard for one night. I was also informed that the ship's name was to be changed from *Cape Agulhas* to *Eastern Sun*. This was great news! On receiving the news, I did not waste any time. I had the same ship chandler who had supplied us with provisions before supplying us once again, and sent in the requisition by email. I was very fortunate this time that there was no boat charge; the owners were paying for the transportation of the surveyor anyway.

The ship chandler brought both the provisions and the surveyor. I had missed out on some important food items in the first supply and prepared another order and had it supplied when the boat returned to take the surveyor ashore. I had to borrow money from my officers again for the second supply.

I sensed that what was happening to me and to the ship was somewhat unusual. I was experiencing bizarre, yet consistent occurrences. Most distressing were the issues with regard to food onboard – issues that I had not experienced in my many years of sea life. It was a disappointing fact that the so-called managers allowed me to endure all these hardships and left me to battle them alone.

There was much fluster with the surveyor suddenly boarding the ship. His entry onboard kept everyone busy. The surveyor spent one night onboard as planned and left the following day. Soon after he left, I sent a message to the owners informing them of the survey and the current situation onboard. A few hours later, I received direct instructions from the owners to proceed to Pointe-Noire in Congo to load. The cargo was part of an oil rig for the purpose of transportation and it was destined for the port of Dar es Salaam in Tanzania.

It was good news for everyone onboard as there were strong indications that the ship would call at Cape Town en route to Dar es Salaam. The ship sailed from Douala anchorage at around 0800 hours on May 13, 2006. The distance from Douala to Pointe-Noire was about 666 nautical miles. It reached the destination in about 48 hours. I was instructed by the port control to anchor at the outer anchorage. When the ship arrived at around 0700 hours on May 15, 2006, it was anchored at out harbor.

During anchor, the charterers wanted the chief officer to come ashore to meet with them and discuss the loading plan. They sent a launch and the chief officer and junior third officer went ashore on it. The officers returned after about five hours and the chief officer briefed me on the quantity of cargo to load and the stowage plan.

While scrutinizing the chief officer's loading plan, I realized that he had not taken into consideration the expected weather pattern after passing Cape Town and around the Cape of Good Hope. He had prepared the loading plan assuming the entire voyage would be under fair weather conditions. I reminded him that he had forgotten a cardinal point on the stowage plan and that the ship will be sailing into very bad weather from Cape Town to about Maputo, Mozambique, via the Cape of Good Hope and Cape Agulhas. I could sense my advice was not welcomed.

From roughly May to September each year, the weather in these areas is anything but calm. Thus, the cargo distribution, especially the loading and stowing of heavy girders and structures, had to be well planned in order to avoid shifting in the side, the holds, and on deck. After scrutinizing the stowage plan prepared by the chief officer, it was necessary to ponder these concerns. I believed that the chief officer had floundered in his professional duties. The attitude that he had taken when planning and preparing this important official document needed to be reassessed. I concluded he had not considered the safety of the lives onboard under stormy weather conditions that could be expected after Cape Town. It appeared that his interest was only up to Cape Town, where a large number of the Myanmar crew would be leaving the ship, himself included.

The attitude of the chief officer certainly did not blend with proper and worthy seamanship. This lapse on his part nudged me to be very wary of his actions and the actions of the crew with regard to the cargo. My years at sea tugged at my internal alarm.

The ship was berthed alongside at around 0730 hours on May 17, 2006. As soon as inward clearance was granted, the loading of cargo commenced. I kept a close check on the intake of cargo and had to amend, on a few occasions, the stowage plan prepared by the chief officer. I could not help but wonder how, after living together like family, he could adopt the attitude of Judas Iscariot. It reached down to my very bones, the feeling that he loathed my observations which he perceived as interference. But the lives of the men onboard were of greater importance than keeping my chief officer happy.

It was around 1500 hours when the PSC officers boarded the ship. It was the same team leader but with two new faces. As soon as they sat down, I told them that the last PSC inspection had been done by them and I had certification of their inspection. They, however, would not listen to me and wanted to carry out a fresh inspection because the ship carried the new name *Eastern Sun*. They began with the usual complaints; there were a multitude of faults, according to them, and I had to go through the same torturous rigmarole again. Suddenly they stopped work and began a discussion in their language.

After a few minutes, the team leader said, "Captain, you have a bigger problem this time; one of the certificates carries the old name." I had already informed Colombo about this lapse, but as usual no action to correct the error had been taken. Thus, it did not take me long to figure out that I was in trouble.

This time, payment had to include their bosses as well. I did not have much cash and they asked for USD 2,000 and said USD 1,000 was for their two bosses.

I did not have a quarter of what they were asking for. Time was running out as they usually finished work at 1700 hours each day.

"Sorry, I do not have any money," I said apologetically.

One of them, a first timer, was very stern and did not want to talk much. When I could not pay them, the leader of the team gave me a form and asked me to sign it. I politely declined to sign it as it was in French and I did not understand the contents. I called the agents on my mobile phone, and the man who was handling our ship told me to accept the form but not to sign it.

They would not give me the form and continued to attempt to force me to sign it. I was very adamant and refused. Their force failed to have any visible effect on me; even if there was an effect, I refused to show it in my face and actions. Annoyed and angry, the four men left the ship. Soon after their departure, I telephoned the MD and explained all that had transpired with the PSC officers.

"John, you could have paid them off and settled the matter," he said, to my exasperation.

"Shaun, you do not send me money to buy provisions, and I am already borrowing from everyone onboard. I already owe the chief officer, the third officer and the chief engineer so much; I cannot ask them for any more, definitely not USD 2,000." "John, try to do something to avoid any detentions and delays," he said without feeling and hung up.

His utterances did not surprise me for I expected such a general and callous statement from him.

On May 18, 2006, at around 1000 hours, the agent arrived onboard and said that his boss wanted to see me. I went with him to his office, and found that the boss was a lady. She was a French national. "Captain, it seems that all of us are in trouble," she said when I walked into her office. She produced a fax message which was written in French and had the English translation as well.

The summary of the message was that the ship was being detained for not having the current name on the Continuous Synopsis Record, which is an official record of the ship's history. The ship was to be detained until the position was rectified. A fine of USD 12,000 had been imposed for non-compliance.

The manager said that she had asked for an appointment with the Director of the Department of Merchant Marine, and said that we needed to go to his office at 1500 hours. As planned, she and I went there. We reached the director's office exactly on-time. When we walked into his office, I saw a man in a suit seated at the desk and another man seated opposite him.

The director was a tall, dark African with a very stately appearance. The other man was the general manager of PSC. He looked much younger when compared with his chief. The lady introduced both officers to me and then sat opposite the director. The general manager moved and sat with me on a couch which was placed opposite the director's desk.

Much of the conversation between the two officers and the manager was in French. I did not understand anything. However, from time to time, certain parts of the conversation were repeated in English so that I could understand. In the meantime, I carried on a negotiation with the general manager separately and he agreed to accept USD 1,500 and withdraw the detention order which had been issued by him. He wanted me to assure him, however, that his boss would not learn of our agreement.

At the first opportunity, I signaled to the manager that I wanted to talk with her in private. A good opportunity for this arose when the two officers walked out of the room indicating that they would be back shortly. Quick to make use of the time alone, I told the manager that the general manager agreed to settle the matter for USD 1,500. She said that this arrangement was fine but we still had to pay half of the fine that had been imposed. This meant that we had to pay USD 1,500 to the general manager and USD 6,000 as the fine.

Under the circumstances, I was happy we managed to get the detention order lifted. The ship would have otherwise been forced to wait in Pointe-Noire for at-least six days until the proper document was sent from Colombo by courier.

When the two officers returned, I thanked them and walked out with the manager. After leaving, she told me, "You know, Captain, I am a married woman with two children. I am here in Pointe-Noire all alone. The rest of my family, my husband and two children are in France. I am here because of my work. The director wanted me to take him out to dinner to reduce the fine, and I agreed to do that. My worry now is I do not know what he will want from me after the dinner." She must have been in her early forties and was very pretty. "What should I do in this situation?"

I thought to myself. I could only pray that God would protect her. These were "occupational hazards and built-in dangers" for her and I desperately wanted to do something, but could not.

As the meeting was on a Friday afternoon, I arranged with the general manager prior to leaving the office that I would meet him later along with the agent's representative. He suggested a restaurant in the city for us to meet at 1000 hours the next day.

The cargo meanwhile was completed and the ship was shifted to another berth.

The next day, I, along with the agent, went to the restaurant as arranged. When we reached the place, I saw the general manager already inside having breakfast. Our discussion was brief; the cash was handed over to him. We also had coffee in the meantime. The general manager told me he did not usually work during the weekend but in order to expedite the matter he would be in his office and would send a fax to the harbormaster, customs, and to the agents informing them that the detention order had been lifted and permission granted for the ship to sail.

He told me that his mother had suffered a massive heart attack and was being treated in a government hospital in his native place, which was about 80 km from Pointe-Noire. Considering that treatment at the facility was lacking in many ways and, because his mother's condition was critical, he said he was worried about her. He went on to confide that the moment work was done, he would hire a vehicle and travel there to meet her and explore all possibilities of transferring her to a private hospital.

I knew that the money was being used to save his mother as good medical care was a primary need in their lives. I could not help but think about the wonder of money. It seemed to be a panacea for all ills.

Soon after, I made my way to the ship and advised the chief officer to check the cargo lashing and to get the crew to do a thorough stowaway search.

We had already had one unforgettable experience, and I reiterated that we would only sail when we were one hundred percent sure that no "unwanted" persons were onboard and cargo was properly secured. The time was around 1300 hours on May 20, 2006. The chief officer informed me that the stowaway check had already commenced and cargo securing was in progress. There were about twenty-eight portable cabins and a few heavy structures including a large Caterpillar generator loaded on the deck. My concern was what action the chief officer would have taken to secure the cargo. I could not place complete trust in him; I could also not do all the important duties on my own without delegating at least a portion of the respective responsibilities.

The number of portable cabins on deck was another cause for concern. It was almost impossible to inspect each and every cabin for stowaways. When I questioned the chief officer about stowaway checks on the cabins he assured me that there was no cause for worry because all cabins had been kept locked and he was in possession of the keys. I had heard many such assurances from him in the past – enough to keep me on pins and needles in the future.

Reliving my past experience with the crew, I allowed about three hours for the stowaway search. At around 1600 hours, the chief officer submitted a signed Stowaway Search Report. Considering the stowaway searches the crew had carried out in the past, I wondered whether the report graciously signed by my chief officer and presented to me had any credibility and meaning. He, however, went on to confirm that the ship was clear of stowaways.

I hoped God would help me keep this assurance alive. There was no way I could delay the ship any further. I called the agents and informed them that the ship was ready to sail and that a pilot could be arranged. I already had the Port Clearance Certificate with me.

The pilot was onboard at around 1700 hours and the ship sailed at 1730 hours on May 20, 2006. The destination was Dar es Salaam via Cape Town. The distance from Pointe-Noire to Cape Town was about 1,838 nautical miles and the distance from Cape Town to Dar es Salaam was 2,480 nautical miles.

The ship started its long voyage and the anticipated crew change at Cape Town promised to make it a very interesting journey.

I had many jobs to attend to: preparing the crews' final wages, preparing final accounts in order to reimburse the money I had borrowed from my officers, preparing provisions and other stores inventories, etc. Despite the heavy load on my mind, I had a somewhat peaceful night's sleep on May 20.

In congruence with the rest of the journey so far, it didn't take long for my peace to be torn asunder. I made my usual visit to the navigation bridge at 0630 hours. The chief officer was the officer of the watch. "Good morning, Chief," I greeted him. "Good morning, Captain," he replied and continued, "We have a problem." What is it now, Chief?" I asked in surprised and curious expectation.

"Last night, between 0200 hours and 0230 hours when the bridge look out man went down for his tea, he saw a black man. Before he could get a good look at him, he disappeared." "That means there is a stowaway onboard?" I asked. I could barely contain my disbelief and anger. There was clearly no point in talking with him about the stowaway checks that were carried out prior to departure. Instead, I said to him, "Chief, I will join you, get all crew except the watch keepers and carry out a thorough check."

I went down to my cabin and prayed to God, and repeatedly asked for pardon for my actions in the past. I asked God to help me and my crew find the stowaway. I knew it would not be easy as we had many portable cabins loaded on deck.

All the deck and engine room crew and officers other than watch keepers were engaged in the search. As we started, the boatswain arrived and reported that someone was knocking from the inside of the hatch access cover of the No. 2 hold. It was locked. I went over there with the chief officer and some of the crew. When we reached the No. 2 hold, the boatswain opened the lock. As he was trying to peep inside, we saw a hand poking out. There were three stowaways in the hold.

By this time, the ship had already steamed for about fifteen hours from Pointe-Noire. If there was any relief to be experienced at the eventual sighting and discovery of stowaways, that relief was certainly not for me. According to the crew member who had seen a stowaway walking stealthily the previous night, he did not resemble any of the discovered stowaways. He had appeared younger.

I advised the chief officer to take care of the stowaways and went to the GMDSS room and sent messages to Colombo and to our agents at Pointe-Noire. I expected advice from Colombo, and as I did not receive any, decided to turn the ship around and go back to Pointe-Noire to disembark the stowaways.

I sent my messages at around 0900 hours on May 21, 2006, but there was no response from the management in Colombo. It was a Sunday and possibly no one had been in the office to see my messages.

The ship had already covered about 200 nautical miles at the point of turning back to Pointe-Noire. Together, the chief officer and I spoke with the stowaways. Two were from Congo and the other was from Nigeria. He spoke to us in English.

The chief officer photographed them and in an effort to complete the standard questionnaire, I interviewed them. The two persons from Congo did not speak English, therefore the Nigerian volunteered to do the translation.

The Nigerian national stated that they were given the impression that cargo onboard the ship was destined for Northern Europe and they planned to take a trip on this ship to get there. For this reason, they had paid the security men at the gate and had entered the port. They had also paid the private security men at the yard inside the port who were tasked with guarding the parts of the rig, including the cabins. Upon receipt of payment, the security men had allowed the stowaways to access one cabin and they had been hiding there the entire time. Once the cabins were loaded, they had anticipated an inspection by the ship's crew and the ports security; after arriving onboard, they had relocated themselves to the No. 2 hold and continued to hide inside the large girders and pipes which were loaded in that hold. Once the hatches were closed and locked it was impossible to stay in and for that reason, they had, one by one, begun to knock at the access door.

When I asked the Nigerian how he got to Pointe-Noire from Nigeria, he said he had arrived there as a stowaway on another ship. He admitted he had expected that ship to go to Europe but it had arrived at Pointe-Noire.

The stowaways were not told at any time that the ship was returning to Pointe-Noire. We decided to leave them with the thought that the ship was bound for Cape Town.

The Nigerian national went on to state that he was twenty-eight years old, and had a degree in commerce. He said that despite his degree, he could not get suitable employment in Nigeria and had worked as a temporary tally clerk for a shipping agent. The money he earned had not been enough to cover his household expenses.

He explained that he was looking after his mother, two younger brothers, and a younger sister. He said that at times he did not have a proper meal for weeks and that he often did not have the money to purchase basic essentials. The cost of living, he told us, was very high. He had been forced to become his family's breadwinner after his father died a few years ago. He begged us not to inform the authorities and said that when the ship reached Cape Town, the three of them would quietly walk off the ship and take care of themselves.

I had another problem on my hands; I needed to locate the stowaway who was still in hiding.

The ship arrived at Pointe-Noire outer anchorage at 0600 hours on May 22, 2006. Immediately upon arrival, the stowaway check resumed. I thanked God when the fourth stowaway was found. He was hiding under a table in a cabin that was loaded in front of the superstructure.

It was later revealed that all four had arrived onboard together. One had remained outside to supply food and water to the others hiding in the hold. It was a great plan until we stumbled upon them.

As soon as the ship anchored, I called the port control and informed them of the stowaways. The agents and the police were immediately dispatched and would be onboard in about 30 minutes. They arrived and boarded the ship. I met them in the officers smoke room. The police officers were armed and two of them went with the chief officer to the cabins wherein we had kept the stowaways. The four were kept in four different locations because I thought we could maintain better control over them; my crew had kept watch over the men.

I instructed the chief cook to provide the agent and the police officers with breakfast. Although they agreed to have breakfast, they changed their minds once they discovered that two of the stowaways were from Congo, more precisely, from the Democratic Republic of Congo. The men were dangerous criminals, wanted men. They had been absconding after allegedly committing two murders. They were arrested immediately and all were taken off the ship. The police officers thanked me for helping them to arrest the two extremely dangerous criminals.

The ship resumed voyage and I thanked God!

Thereafter, I went to check the cargo lashing with the chief officer and boatswain and I was shocked to see the manner in which the cargo was lashed inside the holds and on deck. The lashing was so weak and improper that a slight roll of the ship would cause them to give way; heavy girders and pipes adrift would damage the hull of the ship and allow seawater to rush in. Immediately, the ship would lose stability due to the free surface effect of the water in the holds.

My immediate thought after seeing how the cargo was lashed: this is confirmation of the chief officer's despicable attitude towards both the ship and the safety of the lives onboard. By this time, it had been confirmed that most of the Myanmar crew, including the chief officer, would be signed off at Cape Town. We would be enjoying the good weather off the west coast of Africa all the way up to Cape Town. Thereafter, it would become bad weather, rough to very rough seas associated with heavy swells known as "cape rollers." There was a very good reason for naming the southernmost tip of Africa, the Cape of Good Hope.

By the time the ship made it to the Cape of Good Hope, the chief officer and most of his countrymen would be homeward bound. It would be his blunder – but my responsibility was the lives of the human beings who remained onboard. Fortunately, I became aware of the chief officer's careless and malicious actions in time to prevent grave consequences.

Immediate action was necessary. Therefore, I had no time to waste. I took direct control of planning and the supervision of cargo lashings. Thereafter, I instructed the boatswain and showed him how to carry out proper lashing of the cargo, section by section and hold by hold. When planning cargo lashings, the movements of the ship needed to be considered: rolling, pitching, heaving, and swaying.

I drew some rough sketches and advised on material to use for the lashing – wire ropes, the diameter of the wire, what kind of shackles to use, etc. The boatswain took immediate action. He was a member of the Myanmar crew who requested I retain him as he wanted to stay onboard as long as I was in command.

The weather on the coast of West Africa was good and the crew had ample time to do a thorough job with the lashing. Some of the heavy objects were welded to strong parts of the ship using iron bars and angle iron. I informed the boatswain that he should report to me as I had taken charge and would be personally supervising the lashing. The chief officer already seemed to be on holiday. He followed me around and was a mere spectator. Later that evening, he inquired how much the company would pay as a lashing allowance. "It is a legitimate question, but I have to check with management," I said to him.

On my own I had already decided to pay the crew and two welders USD 1,000. When I informed the chief officer of my decision, he descended and surfaced with a list which had been prepared by him as to how the payments should be made. At the spot which denoted his own name, he had listed USD 250. I declined, and said, "No officer took part in lashing, and no payments will be made to any," I told him. He did not like what he heard, but it was the correct decision, or so I thought. I had listed the highest amount on my list next to the boatswain's name and gave appropriate amounts for the other crew, including the two welders.

I was dissatisfied to the point of disgust with the performance of the chief officer and also with his attitude towards work. But under the circumstances, I had to accept the situation and carry on.

There were a total of twenty Myanmar crew, officers and ratings, onboard at the time. During the voyage to Cape Town, five members of the crew— three from the deck department and two from the engine room department— met with me. This was the first time they came to me as a group, and they informed me officially about their desire to continue as crew for as long as I was the master of the ship. This was very encouraging. I appreciated their confidence in me very much. I told them that once I received written requests from all of them, I would convey their message to the office in Colombo.

After the crew left my cabin, I pondered the situation. Although the MD had indicated repeatedly that he wanted to get rid of all the Myanmar crew, I knew he would like the idea of retaining a few onboard the ship. Judging by his recent actions, if he felt he could save money, he would stoop to any level. Therefore, in order to save on air tickets of both the repatriating and newly-appointed crew, he would want more Myanmar crew to remain and the expenditure to be kept to a minimum.

When I received the five request letters, I sent a message to the MD indicating the requests made by the crew members. He replied in a flash and also asked me to check if there were more men interested in continuing their service.

Was I not right in my thinking?! Not only was I happy, but I wanted the crew members to stay— and contemplated getting more letters.

Anyway, these crew members gave letters confirming their desires. I did not want to squeeze letters out of the others. But I knew if they were not happy and not satisfied with my command, they would not stay. Besides, what better endorsement of my good work than letters from crew members certifying that they wanted to remain onboard with me.

When I sent a message reminding him about the second engineer's matter, he replied stating that it was very difficult to find a replacement and that we ought to let him continue.

"What a wimp the MD is," I thought, and could not accept his decision. The second engineer had tried to assault the chief engineer and had confessed to me that he wanted to finish him off In addition, he had tried to remove the only reliable generator at Cape Town thereby causing the ship to endure further difficulties in the South African coast with two unreliable generators.

The second engineer also had an extreme disregard for the safety and lives of those onboard and I suspected he had ulterior motives which made both him and his decisions dishonorable.

I pondered the attitude of the MD during the next several days and nights. It seemed as though he was always in denial when it came to problems. He refused to accept them, or disputed them, or brushed them aside. Was his judgment impaired by problems he had created around him? His decision-making did not seem to include the welfare of human beings and their well-being.

On May 25, 2006, I sent in my resignation and requested management to sign me off and repatriate me as I could not accept the decisions made by the MD and his staff in general. I was particularly disgusted by the decisions made with regard to discipline and the safety of all lives onboard.

I received a message from the MD on the same day informing me he had changed his original decision and had decided instead to sign off the second engineer. He had also decided not to remove the hired, singly reliable generator until the ship's generators were properly repaired. He also requested that I remain in command of the ship. As I did not trust this man due to past experiences, I did not want to withdraw my resignation.

I also received a message from Colombo informing me that the ship's agent in Cape Town had been changed and that a new agent would be handling the ship during this call. The agent's contact details were given. It was also mentioned that USD 67,000 had been arranged, and provisions and stores would be supplied per the ship's requisitions.

In the meantime, the boatswain and the crew, along with the two welders onboard, did a very satisfactory job of lashing the cargo in preparation for possibly adverse sea-conditions.

The names of the crew joining in were listed but I was surprised to see that the new second engineer's name had been omitted. I sent a message without delay noting that I had already sent three messages listing the breakdown of the cash requirement needed; I had made a request to receive USD 75,000 to settle the wages of the entire crew. I also queried why the incoming second engineer's name was not on the list.

There was no further reply.

At this time, I decided I would not send any more messages but would instead wait and watch the consequences that the company would face if they did not send the correct amount of money onboard.

On May 27, the day prior to our arrival at Cape Town, the chief officer informed me he had instructed all the crew who would be signing off to clean their cabins and make arrangements to shift their bags and belongings to the crew's smoke room so that the new individuals joining in would have access to their cabin. This would allow new members of the crew to occupy the cabins immediately upon boarding and give them a chance to prepare to start work.

I appreciated the chief officer's gesture and thanked him profusely.

The ship arrived in Cape Town on Monday, May 28, 2006, around 0800 hours. It was a nice, clear morning in Cape Town. The Table Mountain and the adjacent areas of the coastline were clearly visible. Port control informed me on arrival that the ship must be anchored outside as there were no berthing instructions. This was bad news.

The ship was at anchorage and I sent a message to the agents.

The agent called me on the VHF and said that he was not aware the ship was arriving today. It appeared to me that the owners had found a fly-by-night, cheap agent who did not seem to have a proper communication system. Because of this fault, the ship remained at anchor for two days and was finally berthed on the third day.

No further information had arrived from management regarding the disposition of a new second engineer. It seemed Mr. Wije would be taking over for the out-going chief engineer. I invited both men to my cabin.

When they arrived, I ushered them to my day room and offered them a drink. I told Mr. Wije, "You must understand, as a senior officer of this ship, that what you have repeatedly done to your colleague is unacceptable under any circumstances. Now that the chief engineer is ready to hand over and leave, first of all, you must apologize to him." He apologized immediately and it was accepted by the chief engineer. I apologized to the chief engineer, and said, "When management dragged their feet over the decision of taking Mr. Wije off the ship, under normal circumstances, I should have resigned. But in this case, because I knew they could not relieve the second engineer it was only a joke putting in my resignation. However, on this issue and on some others, I did put in my resignation. I really wanted to leave the ship. The MD, however, finally agreed to sign off Mr. Wije and also to my other suggestions." The chief engineer was good enough to do a proper handing over to Mr. Wije.

However, a day or so later, the MD requested until Dar es Salaam to sign off Mr. Wije. I wasn't the least bit surprised by the change in plans.

The ship was berthed at around 1700 hours on May 31, 2006. The agent boarded the ship and met with me; the cash received from him was handed over to the chief officer so he could commence payment of the wages to the crew.

The good news was, after so many messages and a few telephone calls, the correct amount of cash had been sent onboard! Immediately after the cash was received, the chief officer with the assistance of the junior third officer, started paying the crew.

The new crew boarded the ship. The new chief officer, a Sri Lankan, came and met with me upon arrival. He informed me that alongside there were two trucks full of various stores and he, together with the new crew, would be taking them onboard.

I later learned that when taking stores onboard, the Myanmar crew had not supported the new crew. Around 2100 hours, the agent called me and informed me that he had received instructions from Colombo that the outgoing crew be retained onboard that night and that they be taken out tomorrow. When I checked with the Colombo office, I learned that this "emergency measure" was because they needed to save money on hotel charges due to financial constraints. I was fully aware of the fact that both sets of crew members would have to rough it for the night. But I remained silent. The situation was beyond my control.

The moment I conveyed the message to the out-going chief officer, the response was immediate; the old crew had gone into their respective cabins and placed the bags of the new crew into the alleyway and resumed occupation of their old cabins. Although this was unacceptable, I refrained from taking any action. This was the most discreet thing to do considering the 'overcrowded' situation onboard and the highly-strung emotional states. The new chief officer had handled the situation well and had informed the new crew that all their belongings would be kept in the officer's smoke room.

The new crew, despite having traveled for nearly two days, had to get on with their work as soon as they boarded the ship. I learned that after all stores were taken onboard, a task that went on until approximately 0200 hours, the new crew then slept in the two smoke rooms. It was a sad and distressing situation.

Brian Perera, the new chief officer, met with me the following morning and told me that the out-going chief-officer had not handed over duties but was ready to leave. He went on to tell me he was confident about getting accustomed to work onboard as he had sailed on the sister ship.

This was very encouraging. "Brian," I said to him, "I can advise you with regard to the cargo onboard as the loading plan and stability calculation was done by me," I added. "As the cargo securing plan was also done by me, you may have nothing to discuss with him," I said.

Considering the situation, I decided not to question the out-going chief officer with regard to his high-handed and unprofessional attitude.

I reiterated to the new chief officer that the most important matter onboard right now was to make sure the cargo lashing was attended to, at regular intervals - not more than twelve hours under normal sea conditions and not more than four hours under bad weather conditions.

The agent arrived at around 1000 hours on June 1, 2006, and took all the crew who had signed off. I was so happy. Finally, I felt I could relax a bit. I called Robert at the local Missions to Seafarers. I remembered he had been very helpful to me during the last stormy call at Cape Town.

Robert came onboard around 1200 noon and I suggested we go out for lunch. He agreed to join me and drove me to an Indian restaurant in town. We had a good, rich, and creamy lunch. The meal gave me a whole new sense of well-being. It was the best meal I had had in a long time.

Thereafter, on my request, he took me to a shopping complex. My mobile phone rang while I was at the mall and the caller was Shaun Gomes.

I was annoyed with him; at first I did not want to answer but immediately changed my mind and answered the call. He sounded very excited. "John, now there is another problem with the bloody signed off crew. They have refused to fly back home in two batches as the agent had not been able to get all on one flight. They are demanding wages for one more day and have already contacted the ITF man there," he said, his voice sounding almost shrill.

"Okay, Shaun," I said. I will go back onboard. But I do not know if I have sufficient cash to pay them," I said. I was so disgusted with him, I couldn't help but continue.

"Shaun, is this the way you run a ship? It is disgraceful. I came to work for a friend, and I am a suffering man today. This stress and suffering are enough for a lifetime," I told him. "Why the hell won't you sign me off, too? Your bloody ship is hell for me and others." He was very quiet and I could almost hear his heavy breathing. "John, I know what you are going through. None of us expected so many problems. Please help me. Try to collect some cash from the crew who received their wages and cover up the shortfall," he said. I did not say a word, but disconnected the line.

The moment I finished the call, I told Robert I had to get back onboard to settle some finances with the crew who had recently signed off. As I was getting into the vehicle, I remembered that the pilot who had berthed the ship had told me that the weather we were currently experiencing was the calm before a storm. In a day or two, there would likely be very bad weather, it was in the forecast. Far away in the southern skies, I could see the conditions for the forecast coming together. My mind raced back to the cargo onboard. I was happy I had personally supervised the cargo lashings and made sure they had been completed.

I thanked God for guiding me.

On arrival, I saw that the entire crew from Myanmar was back onboard. I called the chief officer who had signed off. The first question I asked was why he had left the ship without handing over duties to the new chief officer. It seemed like he had never expected me to ask the question. He could not answer me, possibly because he had no justification for his action, hence he had no answer.

The ITF officer was also onboard. "It seems that you have a great business going on, on this ship." My dig into his character did not need any facial expression. "Where is your famous lawyer?" I continued.

The Myanmar chief officer came to my cabin and apologized to me and to the new chief officer for walking out without properly handing over duties. Then he began his story. "Captain, I am very sorry that we have to trouble you this way. We know what you have gone through during these last four months. This time our problem is that the agent took us to a hotel and asked us to keep our bags in the lobby and then went away. It was around 1400 hours. We asked the hotel staff if we could have lunch there. The front office manager informed me that we could have lunch but we had to pay for it. Captain, you do understand that this is irregular?" he pointed out. He continued on, "I had the cell phone number of the agent so I called and inquired about our lunch. He first said we should pay and have lunch. What I could not accept was that he was very rude to me. He later said he was waiting for approval from Colombo to check us in to the hotel. We have worked hard on this ship and, along with you, have endured all the hardships without making a fuss. Is this the way the company is repaying our gratitude – by throwing all of us out onto the road?" he asked.

It was a sad story, and I detested the irresponsible, demeaning action. We would obviously not like to think it was the work of the ship's local agent and the managers in Colombo.

I immediately prepared an extra day's wages and handed them over to the chief officer to distribute to all of the signed off crew. In addition to a day's pay, I also paid USD 15 for each officer and USD 10.00 for each rating to have a late lunch. I could see the happiness which lit his face. He immediately collected the money and left. In my mind, however, I had not done them a favor; it was their right and dignity that I had restored.

That was the last time I saw those officers and ratings.

I received a notice in the meantime from the harbormaster. The notice said that the weather was expected to deteriorate. All ship movement was to cease from midnight that day. I was not sure whether I was doing the best thing when I informed the port that I would like to sail prior to the ceasing of ship movements. I was aware we would have to go through extremely unfavorable weather conditions from Cape Town until we got to the Mozambique Channel. That was a good six days of sailing.

We had more Sri Lankan crew onboard including an assistant cook. Naturally, we were looking forward to having a typical Sri Lankan-style dinner that day. Luck seemed to be at its lowest. Disappointment reached its peak when the Sri Lankan dinner, too, did not come our way.

The port, adhering to my request, sent the pilot onboard at 1915 hours on June 1, 2006.

I will now take the reader to the navigation bridge of the ship. When I go up on the bridge, I first go through the checklist of what has been completed and signed by the duty officer. Usually that could be either the second officer or the third officer. Like any other prudent master, I do not take the officer's work report to be gospel. Depending on time, I randomly recheck a few of the listed items and also retest certain equipment: manual steering wheel, echo or depth sounder, comparison of compass headings; gyro with magnetic compass, radar, etc.

Having done all of the above, I then check if the departure (as in this case) stations are manned.

Forward of the ship, called forecastle head, are the second officer, bosun, and about three crew members. Aft of the ship, called poop deck, are the third officer, senior able-bodied seaman, and two other crew members.

I check these areas by calling on the portable radio, "Forward, are you ready?" The reply is usually, "Affirmative, Sir," and the same occurs with aft stations.

Thereafter, if the pilot is already onboard, I order, "Standby Engines." The bridge telegraph is brought to "Stand By" position, and engine reciprocating, if they are ready. The time is noted. Usually, it is a time such as 1212, which is divisible by six. There are sixty minutes in an hour and this is done for easy calculation purposes. Helmsman is standby at the wheel. Then I inform the pilot, "Ship is ready."

If there are tugs in attendance, those are made fast. Mooring ropes are taken off, the ship slowly comes out of berth, after clearing the berth and once the vessel is turned towards the harbor entrance, the tugs are cast off. All aforementioned operations are done per the pilot's advice.

The ship sailed out of Cape Town at 1945 hours on June 1, 2006. The pilot disembarked just after clearing the breakwater.

Prior to leaving, he advised, "Captain, I understand that heavy cape rollers are present until you get well past Durban—I suggest you keep hugging the coast until you are north of Durban."

Chapter Nine

Altering the Course

The ship cleared the breakwater and was put on a northerly course. Wind and swell was from the southwest and the ship started to roll heavily to beam sea. Main engine was put on half ahead; the speed maintained was about seven knots. Once the ship cleared the approach channel and other ships at outer anchorage, the course was altered to a westerly course to come out of the bay. The calm only lasted until the ship was altered to a southerly course. The weather was bad and the sea was monstrous outside of Cape Town.

The chief officer came to the bridge and informed me that the cook, who was sailing for the first time, was seasick and vomiting. He was unable to do any work. Fortunately, new deck boys were able to do the cooking. They prepared a palatable dinner. I had had some foodstuff sent from home through the new chief officer and was the lone guest at my own scrumptious dinner. It was a great meal after such a long time.

The weather conditions improved once we left Table Bay. The young third officer, Merril Dias, was the Officer on Watch. Once the ship was well clear of Table Bay, I ordered the engine room to increase speed to maximum sea speed. It was a dark night with overcast skies. The wind was from the southwest. There were swells from three different directions. Observations were made with the help of a signaling lamp, which was quite powerful. I altered course to head south, taking the ship from its initial heading of 270^0 to 230^0, but the ship began to roll violently. I immediately ordered the helmsman to revert to the old course.

After observing the swell, it was decided to alter course, slowly, about five degrees south. It took nearly two hours, but the ship was finally brought to the required course. Manual steering was maintained without the use of the ship's autopilot. There was rolling, but it was not violent.

The crew kept a close watch on the deck cargo lashings. When they inspect the lashings at night, under such conditions, they carry a portable radio and flashlights. A minimum of two crew members carry out the inspection at any given time. They continually report to the bridge; the duty officer is always in contact with them and aware of their position at any given time.

I did not leave the third officer alone on the bridge for long periods as he was very scared of the weather conditions at that time. On the following day, once we cleared Cape Agulhas, the third officer said, "Sir I was watching you closely during the first watch— how you were altering the course without letting the ship roll violently. Believe me sir, I was very frightened. I have never experienced such a high and confusing swell."

He was right, and I was too engaged in my duties to analyze my own actions. I appreciated the third officer's observation.

During the southern winter, from about June to September, the weather in the south coast of Africa is very severe, the worst being around Cape of Good Hope and Cape Agulhas. The decision to close the port was due to an approaching cold front, a mass of cold air, which was the prelude to a frontal depression.

Cape Agulhas is derived from the Portuguese name *Cabo das Agulhas*, meaning Cape of Needles. Geographically, the location is the southern tip of the African continent. It is also considered the beginning of the dividing line between the Atlantic and Indian oceans. Historically, the cape was known as a major hazard on the traditional clipper route due to the treacherous reef. Even in the modern age of large ships with sophisticated navigation systems, travel in this area during southern winter could easily become hazardous.

During the first night, I observed swells from three different directions. One such swell was distinctly high; it was known as a cape roller.

I went to sleep at around 2330 hours on June 1, 2006. Although the ship was rolling heavily, I thanked God we were now out of the most dangerous area. I always try to explain to my junior officers the maneuvers that can be exercised in times of dangerous sea conditions. I distinctly remember learning from books and from observing the actions of my masters and senior officers. I felt it was very important to impart my knowledge to my junior officers. I believed that this was the only way they, too, could become educated and made fearless. Looking back on innumerable casualties at sea, a large number of deaths were caused by panic and the unskilled actions of seafarers.

The ship was sailing around the cape when I went on the bridge at around 0600 hours on June 2, 2006. Although the weather was not as bad as the previous night, the ship was rolling heavily and violently at times. It was taking cape rollers on the beam.

Following the advice of the pilot who had sailed the ship out of Cape Town, and drawing from my past experiences in the region, I brought the ship very close to the coast in order to avoid the effects of the cape rollers. There was a considerable improvement after the deviation of course.

About a day after passing Durban, we experienced fairer weather conditions. After sailing into good weather it appeared that the new crew were settling in. However, we seemed to be having problems with the new cook. He was, in fact, the assistant cook. The person who signed on as chief cook had not been allowed to leave the country by Sri Lankan immigration authorities. Apparently, he had a pending court case.

This was causing quite a problem to all aboard. A discussion with the assistant cook revealed he was versant only in the making of fried rice and bites. I noted with consternation and surprise that he could not prepare even a simple meal of rice and curry. I instructed the chief officer to arrange a meeting of all officers and ratings. It was during the meeting that some of the new crew revealed that the company had charged them the return airfare from Cape Town to Colombo.

It was clear that the MD's principles and policies were on a questionable trend. It was both disgusting and disappointing to learn that the company had taken money from the crew members and some of the officers in order to get to the ship's location. When monies were being charged, how could one expect an exceptional crew? Sea ratings from Asian countries are poorly paid. For the company to take money from them to be signed on the ship was perhaps the lowest depth of money-making. The measly earnings of the ratings from Sri Lanka were not enough to give their folks back home a comfortable existence. Limited by their remuneration, they were unable to buy the gifts they wanted to give their loved ones. Their helplessness was heightened when their bank reserves depleted with each passing week.

Many of them were in debt. Money had been borrowed at very unethical and unbelievable rates of interest just so they could pay the company to get to the ship. Here they were, slogging away, surrounded by deprivation and hard work just so that they could pay back these high rates of interest.

The meeting went on for about two hours. The predicament of the newly joined Sri Lankan second engineer came to light. He was recently married and had agreed to join the ship under the condition that his wife could sail with him. Onboard, the reality of sailing was everywhere. It was visible in the form of cockroaches; they were on his bed and in his cabin. Beads of sweat and creaking were facts of life. Sadly, it was his assignment to sail as an engineer. The circumstances were not ideal; if marriages were made in heaven, this one would certainly be started in hell.

In addition, we had another stowaway onboard. We seemed to have a cocktail of misfortunes and problems— a stowaway, an assistant cook with few skills, and the biggest bombshell of them all: a fuel shortage onboard which wasn't noticed until there was a comparison between figures provided by the last chief engineer and the actual figures obtained once the ship entered calmer weather.

Every dark cloud has a silver lining, however. The good news was that fuel reserves were sufficient to reach our destination. However, fuel resources needed to be rechecked and confirmed once the vessel arrived inside the port of Dar es Salaam.

Mr. Wije claimed that the previous chief engineer had received a lesser quantity of fuel than noted when the bunkers were replenished mid-sea on the way to Malabo. It also became known he had sold some fuel oil along with the sludge at Douala.

Fuel oil was used in the main engine when the ship was out of port until maneuvering commenced. Diesel oil was used for maneuvering the ship to bring it into the port and berth.

I informed the agents in Colombo and Dar es Salaam, as well as the charterers, that our expected time of arrival was 0900 hours on June 9, 2006.

I expected no applause for our hard work and dedication during the most trying of conditions. Instead, I received a very nasty message from Colombo mentioning the possible shortage of heavy oil. In the same message it stated that the acting chief engineer would be signed off at Dar es Salaam. I copied the message to the acting chief engineer. He was moved by the nasty message—his anger, disgust, and annoyance were clear.

It did not take me hours to analyze the situation. I knew that Mr. Wije, too, was responsible for the issues that had arisen over the fuel shortage scenario. I had suggested many time to Colombo to sign off Mr. Wije, but the MD kept dodging the issue. Now it seemed there was little choice; Mr. Wije, the acting chief engineer, had to be removed.

The ship arrived at the Dar es Salaam anchorage at around 09:00 hours on June 09. The port traffic control advised me to drop anchor at the outer anchorage and wait for berthing instructions.

I sat and thought about Dar es Salaam. I had been there previously and remembered its extensive natural harbor. Dar es Salaam means "haven of peace" in Arabic. It was the largest city in Tanzania and an important economic center on the Swahili coast.

We did not have to wait long at the anchorage. At around 1800 hours, PSC called the ship and asked me to get it underway and approach the pilot boat. After a few minutes of river passage, the ship arrived at the allocated berth. At 1915 hours, on arrival at berth, the stowaway was removed by the local police.

Thereafter, I encountered a grave problem with regard to the presence of cockroaches onboard. I accepted the cockroach problem, but what I could not accept was two quarantine officers' demands for a bribe of USD 1,000 to grant clearance. It was far too much to pay for cockroaches. I negotiated with the officers and paid them USD 600. With that settled, quarantine clearance was granted.

It was 2000 hours by the time all typical port formalities were completed, and the ship was granted inward clearance.

The agent told me he would arrange a vehicle if I needed to go out. I inquired where I could go to listen to music and have a wholesome meal. He suggested a particular place by the beach. He also told me that the place was about nine km from the port. He advised that I retain the vehicle so that I could return to the ship.

Mr. Wije was looking forward to being signed off at Cape Town. I received a message on arrival at the port, however, that he would be signed off in Dar es Salaam. His relief, another Sri Lankan chief engineer, was due to board the vessel the following day.

In the meantime, Mr. Wije brought more bad news. I realized that for the four months he had been onboard as the second engineer, and subsequently as the acting chief engineer, he had never been the bearer of good news. The bad news this time was that the shortage of heavy fuel had been confirmed.

Our fuel situation was dire.

Chapter Ten

A Farewell at Q-Bar

Despite the fuel oil problem and considering the good times we had had during Mr. Wije's tenure onboard, especially his preparation of wonderful meals for us, I decided to take him out for the evening. It was a farewell for an officer who had, on several occasions, cooked and provided us with palatable food. With my plan in mind, I called him to my cabin and invited him to join me. He told me he did not have any money to spend. I assured him I would take care of all expenses. "Mr. Wije, get ready, and then come back. I will be here," I told him.

After Mr. Wije left my cabin, I pondered my carefree sailing days and life spent as a junior officer in different posts. Life itself is like the sea—endless different waves to pass through before reaching one's destination. Thereafter, I had a shower and got ready for the evening. It was around 2100 hours when Mr. Wije and I got into the car and headed out to an unknown destination. Fortunately, the driver spoke some English and I asked him the best place where we could listen to some live music and have a drink. He told us there was a place by the beach and he would take us there. I asked him to call and check with the agent to see if it was the same place he had suggested. We received a message: yes, it was the same venue.

After driving along bumpy roads for about thirty minutes, he turned the vehicle into a narrow by road. The driver announced that he was taking us to a place called the Q Bar. It did not take long before the vehicle was driven into the car park of a large restaurant by the beach. The moment the vehicle entered the premises, I could hear the sound of live music. I could sense a ray of happiness rest upon me. I looked at Mr. Wije and saw his eyes light up with delight.

The driver walked with us to the entrance and met with a gentleman, who was the manager of the Q-Bar. Our agents, especially William, the boarding officer who arranged the vehicle, were acquainted with the manager. After introducing us, the driver told me he would return to the car and wait.

We were taken inside and shown to a table about ten to fifteen meters away from the bandstand, but we had a clear view of both the band and the dance floor. After we took our seats, the manager told me he would be around if I needed him, and then he went away.

I did not waste any time for the fun to begin. I gave our order to the attending waitress. I ordered Castle Lager, a South African beer, for both of us. I observed around us only a few men but many women of different complexions.

Mr. Wije was about 4 feet, 8 Inches in height, dark in complexion, and of medium build. He always bragged about the different pretty women he had been out with before marrying his beautiful wife. He had told the entire crew of the ship that he was an expert in martial arts. It had been reported to me, on a few occasions, that he had pulled out iron bars to assault people onboard, especially the previous chief engineer. I often wondered why an expert in martial arts had to depend on an iron bar to attack an opponent.

My mind was wandering. Why was I thinking of Mr. Wije and his iron bar when the music was tantalizing and the women were mesmerizing? Mr. Wije was more animated after a few drinks and bolder, too. He invited a girl to join him. Observing his demeanor, I thought, "This man talks so much of the love he has for his wife and family, but yet he cannot resist the company of a woman just twenty-four hours before he reaches home!" But he was enjoying himself and I was truly happy for him. A little while later, another girl joined him; he had his arms around both of the girls. At this time, I inquired of him, in our native language, what his intentions were.

He said that he had some money, a few US dollars borrowed from another officer. He said that he would take care of the expenses of the girls. I told him that as long as it was only drinks and food for the girls, I would pick up their tabs.

When we had spent about an hour and half in the restaurant, I suddenly saw four crew members from our ship walk in. When Mr. Wije learned of this, he wanted to leave and go to another place. I did not think it was necessary for us to leave the place. But I could sense that my compatriot did not want to continue having fun with two girls by his side. I settled the bill immediately, and stood up to leave. My crew saw and acknowledged us, but they did not come closer. Perhaps they did not want to embarrass the chief engineer.

Suddenly, Mr. Wije threw a fresh problem into the mix. "Captain, these women do not want to come with me to another place but are asking me for payment for keeping me company," he said in distress. He did not want to give them any money so we left the place. When we returned to the car, the driver was somewhat surprised. He did not expect us to leave that early. I explained the situation to him, and he agreed to take us to another place nearby.

While driving, he told me, "Sir, some crew from your ship came in a taxi and had a fight with the taxi driver." It had apparently been over a controversy about the taxi fare. "The taxi driver pulled a knife out and I shouted out to him; he nearly stabbed one of them. That taxi driver left but I am sure he will be back," the driver said. I asked him what should have been the taxi fare?

He said that it would be around 10,000 Tanzanian Shillings (TZS), equivalent to about twelve US dollars.

I knew that they did not have this amount of money; the four men had just joined the ship. After I heard what the driver had to say, I was very happy we had left that place. After driving for six to seven minutes, the driver brought us to another restaurant. I found that it was very quiet there. There was no music. We were greeted by a dull atmosphere and there were only four people patronizing the place. I consoled myself by saying that we did need some peace and quiet to overcome the "happenings" of the last hours; I ordered myself a beer.

When we were well into the second round, Mr. Wije said that he would ask the driver to go and see if our ship's crew were still at the other place. I told him he could use my mobile phone to call the driver and pass along his message. Mr. Wije explained his request to the driver. The driver said that it was not necessary to actually go there; he could call the manager on the phone and ask him whether the people were still around. The news was good for Mr. Wije. The other members of the crew had settled their bill and were about to leave the place. Hearing the good news, Mr. Wije was very excited. Meanwhile, I settled the bill and we walked back to the car.

We were back in the old place within a few minutes. I could sense Mr. Wije's anxiety; he was doubling his walking speed. Fortunately, we got the same table and the two girls came back. Mr. Wije was a happy man again.

We had been drinking for several hours yet had not eaten anything. I ordered some food for the girls as well. I went to the washroom and as I was returning, a girl came up to me and began to talk to me in Hindi. "Are you from India?" she asked me. "No I am from Sri Lanka," I said. Then she went on to ask how I spoke Hindi. "I have studied in India, lived in India and worked with Indians," I explained.

She showed me a vacant table and asked me if she could talk to me. I did not want to appear rude. But, before I consented, I said, "I do not know what you have in mind and what you are trying to tell me. I am ready to listen to you but please note that I am not looking to take you out for the night. I am with a colleague," I said, pointing to where Mr. Wije was seated. I signaled to him and indicated that I would be sitting here for a few minutes. When I did this, I saw him rise from his chair and walk over to me. He appeared to be walking on cloud nine. "Captain, you have good taste," he chuckled. I did not want to say anything to him at that point in time, so I simply accepted his statement.

I asked the girl her name. After a short pause, she said, "They call me Mona in this place. But, my real name is Reema, Reema Doshi." "Reema, what can I get you to drink?" I asked her. "Any soft drink or bottled water, please," she replied. I reiterated to Reema that I had no intention of using her services, if that was her ultimate intention. "You wanted to talk to me and I am ready to spend about fifteen to twenty minutes until our dinner is served," I told her.

There was fun and excitement in the air and it was in this spirit, I think, that Mr. Wije sent a bottle of beer to my table. I ordered a bottle of Coke for Reema. Reema, to family and friends. Mona, to the customers.

"I was watching you walking towards the washroom," she said softly. Suddenly, she began to talk in English and the rest of the conversation was in English. She spoke fluently. Reema began to relate her story to me as the evening progressed.

She asked me for my name. "I am John," I said. Then she asked what brought me to Dar es Salaam. "I am a captain of a ship and the ship is in the port," I said. "From the time I saw you, I wanted to talk with you. I was positive that you were an Indian!" she said, almost sighing. "Captain, I do two jobs in this place. I will explain everything. Please listen to me".

"I have been suffering deep down in my very being for a long time. I think God has sent me the right person so that I can pour my heart out. You made it very clear to me that you have no intention of using me for paid sex," she said sadly. "My family was originally from Gujarat, India, and they were business people in Dar es Salaam. I had my primary education in a missionary school. I joined college thereafter. In college, I fell in love with a

Tanzanian student. He was a Muslim. Our love affair grew to such an extent that I started going out with him occasionally, despite my conservative culture. We spent a lot of time in parks, and went to movies, too. Once, after a movie, he invited me to visit a friend. I very reluctantly accepted his invitation. Although I expected to go to a house, he brought me to a guest house in the city, where a friend of his worked. While I was seated in the lobby, my boyfriend, Hassan, went looking for his friend. Upon his return, I saw some keys in his hand. Thereafter, he took me to a room," she recollected. "Hassan, why are we here? Why did you want to get a room? We could have had a conversation somewhere outside, as usual," I told him. "But he would not listen to me. He then pushed me onto the bed and made love to me. I lost the most precious thing in my life. He did not rape or force himself on me; he made love, with my consent.

On that day, I went home quite late, with tears of sadness, anger, and disgust in my eyes. I cursed myself as I had let myself lose the most sacred state of a young girl — her virginity. When I walked into the house, I was filled with guilt. My parents loved me and cared deeply for me. They had high hopes for me and my brother. On that day, I had to make up a string of lies as to why I was late. Yet, I had to listen to the berating of my parents and my brother," she said.

"I could not get rid of that 'dirty' feeling. I was awake the whole night through. My mother saw that I was awake and asked what was bothering me. What could I tell her? I could not break her heart. It was best that I suffered my own misfortune alone."

I thought to myself how it took only a few minutes to destroy the happiness of this intelligent, pretty young girl who had had everything.

"I got pregnant. When I found out, I begged Hassan to take me somewhere because I did not want my parents to learn of my condition; especially not my father. He took me to his village, which was in the interior and was about 160 km from here. When we reached his home, his mother welcomed both of us. His father was not in the house at that time. According to their standards, they were people of high society in that village. The family owned a local bar and a grocery shop," she elaborated. "However, I found that their style of living was very different to that of ours, and I just could not stay. The main problem was communication. His mother did not speak English and the father could just manage to convey his message. Although both of them appeared to be rough people, they were quite humble in their own way. There were distinct indications that I was not welcome to the family as I was not a Muslim. As there was no other alternative, I endured all that came my way until the baby was born," she said.

Thereafter, we returned to Dar es Salaam with some money we received from Hassan's father. We never got married. Hassan found a job as a steward in a restaurant. We moved into a one-room flat and started over life together. After about a year, my boyfriend suddenly disappeared. I looked all over for him. Carrying my little child, I walked for miles each day. I did not have money to pay the rent and feed the baby. I went to the restaurant a few times, but none of his colleagues told me what happened to him or where he had gone. Subsequently, when I met with the manager, he told me Hassan had left the restaurant and had gone back to his native place," she explained.

"I went all the way to his native home, carrying our child with me. Weathering all the odds, I reached his home. It was strange the way these people treated me. I lived with them for such a long time and now they did not seem to have even a smile for me. To them, I was wreckage from the past. It was a long, back-breaking distance to travel, and I begged them to let me stay the night. No one would tell me where Hassan was. In the night, too, my eyes searched for him outside," she said, with tears in her eyes.

"On the following morning, when I was ready to leave the house, Hassan's mother gave me some money. I later found that there were about 10,000 Tanzanian shillings in the money she squeezed into my hand. I returned to Dar es Salaam, and a few weeks later found a job working as a saleswoman in a shop owned by a Yemeni family. I started work at 8:00 a.m. each day and sometimes worked until about 7.00 p.m. During the time I was away from home, my child was looked after by the reverend sisters in a convent.

They were very helpful to me. Sometimes they even gave me food to take home, and did not charge me for their services."

"One month or so after I began working in the shop, the owner's wife and family went on a holiday to Yemen. I had to go to their house very early and pick up the shop key from my boss. Thereafter, I opened the shop, swept, and cleaned before he came to work. Once, when I went to his house, he called me in and embraced me.

Then he began to kiss me and thereafter had sex with me. He wanted me to come to his house every evening, after closing the shop. As I had to protect my job, I did all that he wanted me to do. He was about fifty-five years old, and a man of large build. It was a nightmare. I found that not only was he suffering from bad breath, but he was not fanatical about washing and cleaning himself. The sex was violent, leaving me with bruises," said Reema.

Continuing her desperate saga, she said "After I started visiting my boss's house every day, it was about 9:00 p.m. when I went to the convent to pick up my child— on some days, it was even later than that. The reverend sisters questioned me as to why I was late. A bad situation became worse when the sister-in-charge observed a red patch on the right side of my neck, and wanted to know what had been its cause.

They suspected I was going elsewhere after work; they refused to look after my child anymore.

That was the end of my greatest solace, a safe place for my child while I worked," said Reema.

"Soon, I began to think that was enough— what I had already gone through with my boss was too traumatic for me. I stopped going to work in the shop. But I needed to pay my day-to-day expenses. After a great deal of thinking, I decided to come to this place and ask the manager for some work."

In Reema's case, she had been forced into sex in two different instances, although the word "rape" could not be used. In the latter case, not only was she forced, but also had to endure revolting situations.

It's possible that Reema could have averted the selfish and malicious acts of these persons in both cases. She had gone into these situations, walked into them innocently, and had come out scathed for life.

Reema's story continued. "The present manager of this place was the assistant manager at the time my boyfriend worked here. He knows my story. When I met with him, he said he could not employ me on a permanent basis. However, he said he would help me with some temporary work on busy days: Thursdays, Fridays, and Saturdays," she said. "Thereafter, I began to come here. I come here every evening and on some days, I get work in the kitchen, for which I get paid about 2,500 TZS (about USD 2) for a day. On other days due to the dire straits I am in, I go with a customer and I earn about 15,000 TZS (about USD 7). My average monthly income is about 100,000 TZS. This is barely enough income to cover basic expenses, but there is no other way out of the scarcity, want, and suffering," she explained.

In the midst of this story, Mr. Wije came to us two or three times to remind me that the food had already been served. I invited Reema to join me at our table, and I told her to have my dinner. After seeing the two girls who were seated next to Mr. Wije, she told me, "I am not in that group; those girls will not like me joining you." "I decide here, not them. You come and have dinner," I told her.

She did not have the dinner but said that she would wrap the food and take it home. I understood. Mothers always think of their children first when good things come their way.

All that she was going through were the consequences of one wrong relationship. It was relevant to my life at that time; too, for here I was facing the consequences of going my own way after ignoring the Word of God.

During the extra time Mr. Wije had been with the girls, he had had quite a few beers and had paid for those extra indulgences.

It was time to leave and after settling the final bill, I gave Reema 10,000 TZS. The other two girls saw this gesture and asked Mr. Wije for money. They pestered him so much that he pulled out some dollars and gave the notes to them. It seemed that there were about USD 18. First, both girls had a massive argument over the sharing of the money. They turned to Mr. Wije and demanded more money! It was not the nicest situation to be in— in the midst of two women, fighting over a man for money.

Reema was watching all this. I got so angry, I pulled the money away from their hands and gave it to Reema. The two girls disappeared and Reema thanked us both and left. When the both of us were walking towards the vehicle, suddenly, the two girls appeared with a policeman. He had a machine gun in his hand. He began to talk to us in the native language and we did not understand anything. Our driver had been watching the entire situation and came to our rescue. He spoke with the policeman and explained to us that the policeman wanted us to come with him to the police station. "What is that for? Why do we have to go to a police station?" I asked him. The driver told me that the girls had made a complaint, and that was why he wanted us to come and meet the officer-in-charge.

As there was no other alternative, we agreed to proceed to the police station. I was wondering for what reason we had to go to a police station. Our driver, in the meantime, had informed the agent's boarding officer, William, about what was happening.

The girls were taken in a jeep and we went in our car. We reached the police station in about five minutes. We got out of the car and walked inside. The three cops who were in the jeep came in along with us. None of them spoke English. When our driver, Ibrahim, came into the police station, one cop said something to him in the local dialect. It was presumed that he was asked to leave. Ibrahim signaled to me and confirmed that he was asked to leave. This was bad news. I asked the officer, who appeared to be the senior, "Why were we called to the station? We went to Q-Bar and had a few drinks and dinner. Those two girls were also given drinks and dinner and none of us had anything to do with them. Drinks and dinner were given to them because they kept us company. What is the problem now?"

From the corner of my eye, I saw the girls sobbing and talking with another officer.

After listening to me the officer asked me if I had any cigarettes. I said, "No, I do not smoke. Therefore, I do not carry any cigarettes." Then he asked if I had any US dollars. When I said "No," he asked for some local money. I then gave him about 15,000 TZS.

While I was dealing with the policeman, I watched Mr. Wije— he was so drunk that he could barely stand.

I prayed to God and asked for His help.

A little while later, a person in civvies walked into the police station and went straight into a room. Thereafter, he called the policeman who called us to the station in the first place.

After about fifteen minutes, he came out of the room and asked, "Who is the Captain?" "I am the Captain," I said. Then he called me and Mr. Wije to his room and wanted to know what happened. I explained everything in detail.

"Is it stated in the law of this country that if anyone talks to a girl in a nightclub or restaurant that it is mandatory that he has to pay the girl?" I queried. "There is no such thing, but those girls are very poor. They come from different parts of Africa. So they expect to earn some money," he said. "It is alright; you can go now. Sorry for bringing you here and keeping you. As for the girls, I shall produce them in court tomorrow for being a nuisance and disturbing the peace," he said.

I thanked God. Thereafter, I thanked the officer and left the police station.

On our way back, the driver, Ibrahim, told me that the officer-in-charge of the station was well known to William. It was William who had called in his friend who had arrived at the station to attend to our squabble.

I pondered on all that had happened, and came to the conclusion that I had to endure all these difficulties because I had chosen to ignore God's word. If that was the case, then what was next, I thought.

I was happy to be back on board after the evening's problems. I paid USD 50 to Ibrahim and asked him to come back the following day to take me out again. While walking up the gangway, Mr. Wije said, "Captain, you did not have dinner. I am sure you must be very hungry." "Mr. Wije, I am very hungry, but that's okay," I said.

The pangs of hunger were gnawing at my stomach and abdomen, but too much had happened during the evening. I was moved by Reema's story. My thoughts were on the poor girls who were forced to work the nights. It was a sad and unfair world. No, it was not the beer that was making me melancholy.

Mr. Wije came with me to my cabin, and said, "Captain, I will go down and prepare something for you. Can you wait for about half an hour?" I was very happy. "Thanks, Mr. Wije," I said. "I will most certainly wait," I added.

I opened a bottle of chilled beer and, to keep my eyes open, switched on the TV and played some music. While I was watching a musical VCD, Mr. Wije returned with the food. He had made devilled chicken. We continued drinking and looking back at the happenings of the night. We ended up at a Tanzanian Police station, but for doing what? That was a question we could not answer.

The session of drinking continued till 0230 hours the next day, after which we shared the food.

Finally, when I went to bed, I could not fall asleep. My thoughts were deep into Reema's story. Her parents were in Dar es Salaam, why couldn't she go and explain the situation to them? Surely no parent would throw their anguished child to the streets, whatever his or her faults may be. I prayed, and just before I fell asleep, I decided to meet with her and persuade her to go back to her parents.

I received a message from Colombo the following morning, advising me to proceed to Mombasa, Kenya for bunkers. I immediately called the second officer and asked him to check if we had the required charts to approach Mombasa. He returned after a few minutes and told me that we did not have the required charts. When I informed Colombo, I received an interesting reply. The message said, "Buy the charts. If they are not available; try to borrow from another ship in port." How educational! What original and innovative instructions!

From the very beginning, this was the type of message I received from the so-called managers in Colombo.

I had no other alternative but to call the agents and ask them for help by way of arranging a vehicle— and for someone to accompany my second officer to visit other ships in port for the purpose of trying to buy or borrow the required charts. They obliged.

There was a car, and William himself was there to take my officer to other ships to hunt for charts. "Captain, there are four other ships in port which are under our agency. I will take the second officer to those ships," said William.

The second officer returned after about two hours and told me that two ships had the charts but did not want to sell them as they did not have extras. However, they had agreed to let us take the charts and photocopy them and return the originals thereafter. Unfortunately, we found that there were no facilities available to photocopy the complete chart. Therefore, each was separated and photocopied on A4 paper, and then taped together.

Chapter Eleven

Choosing the Right Path

I have been to Mombasa three times since I assumed my first command in May, 1990. What is of greater significance now is not how many times I have navigated ships into the port but how many times I have had the required and current navigational charts and other publications that cover the port of Mombasa. Safety of the crew onboard, the ship, and the environment is of paramount importance. It should definitely not be a heroic act of a ship master to navigate a ship to a port under bad weather conditions without proper charts. Unfortunately, we had already received weather messages indicating bad weather was ahead. The forecast warned of inclement weather with gale force winds and rough seas.

I am not a captain who deviates from accepted norms and courses. But I am guilty of irregular action from time to time; these deviations occur for the interest and well-being of the others around me. I wanted to keep the ship moving from place to place. My method for doing so called for intrigue. I was trying to once again make the best of a bad situation.

I always expected Shaun Gomes and his senior staff members to review the whole scenario and recognize that I was doing an honorable job. But it looked like I would have to wait until the cows came home for that recognition to arrive. When in a moving ship, there is no waiting. Every minute mattered. Every day mattered.

On June 10, 2006, around 1000 hours, while I was sitting alone in my cabin and pondering, William walked in. "Captain, I have some bad news for you," he said. "William," I told him, "your bad news will only add to the stock that I have gathered during the last four months anyway, so please break it to me." "Captain," he said, "today is Saturday and your owners have not yet paid our agency fees and other expenses. Even if the ship completes discharging during the weekend, my boss has decided to detain it until we get our money." "That is not bad news to me," I laughed, "on the contrary; it is good news, for we will then have more time to look for the required charts."

I invited William to go to dinner with me. He accepted my invitation, and said that he would be onboard by 1900 hours.

I felt a nagging need to meet Reema again and suggest to her that she ought to go back to her parents. I was also toying with the idea of taking her back myself.

Mr. Wije was leaving the ship that evening and his relief was already onboard. The new chief engineer was Jerry Anthony, a Sri Lankan. Mr. Wije came along with him and introduced him. He left thereafter to do his last minute packing. Meanwhile, Jerry and I had a long talk.

During our conversation, I updated him on many important matters concerning the ship's engine room, especially the condition of the auxiliary engines. Jerry made certain statements that made me laugh out loud. It appeared Shaun Gomes and his crew manager had bombarded this poor man with lies and persuaded him to join the ship. I was very careful, however, when talking with the new chief engineer. The last thing I wanted to do was to upset this hopeful man on his very first day onboard.

I got ready for the evening at around 1830 hours. William was onboard at 1900 hours sharp. I met Mr. Wije prior to departure and bid him goodbye. He was not a great engineer, and his bad temper heightened his professional shortcomings. Nevertheless, owing to him, we had had some good food from time to time. He took on the cooking tasks with great results until the Sri Lankan cook arrived. The last supper Mr. Wije had cooked, the great food from the previous night, had been memorable. The taste still lingered on my tongue.

I expressed to William a desire to go to the same restaurant that I had patronized the day before. When I told him this, he had a devastatingly mischievous smile on his face. I did not want to discuss that smile. We left the ship around 1930 hours, and reached the restaurant in about twenty minutes.

I saw Reema just as soon as I walked in. She came running up to me, "Captain," she said, "I thought that you would not set sight on this place again after yesterday's unpleasant incident." "Reema," I replied, "what happened yesterday is now history. Meet my friend William." She was very uncomfortable when she realized that William was a Tanzanian. The presence of William impaired Reema's candor. I told her that my visit to the place today was particularly to have a discussion with her, to find a permanent solution to her problem. She was ready to talk but had reservations due to William's presence.

William, sensing the discomfort in the air, said "Captain, I have to go and meet the manager, my friend." "Okay, but do not take long," I responded.

Basking in the newly found freedom, Reema's eyes lit up with expectation. She seemed very happy at that moment. "This is not a life to live. You are only about twenty-one years old. Think of your family. In your mind you have created a situation that if you go home, your father and brother would kill you. I think it is better to die at your father's hand than to sell your body to earn a living." I tried hard to convince her.

During the time I spent with her, I was tempted, on many occasions, to have sex with her. But I feared God and remembered His words in the scriptures. I silently prayed, asking for God's help to resist temptation which would have been induced by Satan. In situations of this nature, when a person asks for help from God, the Holy Spirit acts on the person and he is relieved from such temptations.

That was exactly what happened to me. I always thought to myself, "I have a good family. Whatever I do in this place, my wife or my children will never know. But how can I hide all this from God?"

I explained to Reema a little bit about the scriptures and said that was why I did not use her services. "It is adultery and it is sin. I am trying my best to live without getting into sin anymore," I told her as she listened intently. "I realized that the more alcohol I have in my system, the more prone to sin I am," I explained. "It is the same with you. I have only tomorrow. Let me talk to your parents and make arrangements for you and your child to go back to them," I appealed to her.

"Captain, I do not want to go, especially because of my brother. He will definitely make the matter worse. All that is owned by our parents was for both of us. Now that I have left the family, he must be very happy and comfortable. Why should I go back and disrupt their peace and happiness?" she asked. "Reema, don't talk nonsense," I said. "Give me the telephone number of your home,

I will call them now. It is not that late, it is only about 8:30 p.m."

She was reluctant to give me the telephone number, and began to give me various excuses. "Okay," I said, "do not give me the number of your parental home but give me your address and the address of your shop." "It is very easy to find our shop because the 'National Emporium' is one of the biggest shops in town. It is a department store in the heart of the city," she said. She gave me her address and the name of their shop. I saw a mobile phone in her hand and I took down the number of her telephone.

Thereafter, I did not discuss the matter any further. I asked her what she would like to eat. "I will order something like yesterday, pack and take it home. Once the food is ready, I will leave and await a call from you tomorrow," she said. "I am very fortunate to have met with you, and I thank God for that," she said as she was leaving, sincerity and emotion written all over her face. "I, too, thank God for giving me the patience and wisdom to handle this matter," I responded.

Reema collected her food and left. I could see the tears glistening in her eyes and on her cheeks.

When William rejoined me I thanked him for his consideration. I told him briefly of the bizarre happenings in Reema's life. I also requested he join me to go to her shop, the "National Emporium."

That evening, I may not have been great company to William. My mind was preoccupied with planning a solution, a permanent, comfortable settlement for Reema which would lift her out of her nightmare. It was, however, a nice evening with live music setting the tempo for a good dinner.

I returned to the ship at about 2300 hours and could not sleep that night, either. I was up at 0400 hours and started the day after a cool refreshing shower to liven my groggy mind. When I checked my messages there was one from Shaun Gomes. He had advised me to proceed to Salalah after Mombasa.

Salalah is a port in the southern part of Oman. The purpose of call was to make the ship available for a prospective charterer to carry out an inspection. As this was in the pipeline prior to arriving at Cape Town, all the required charts had been ordered and received. While acknowledging the message, I mentioned that I needed to be relieved on arrival at Salalah, as I had fully completed my contract with the company by that time. The contract was for four months.

My chief officer made his customary visit at 0700 hours on June 11, 2006. The discussion that I had with him continued until breakfast time. He told me that the receivers of the cargo and the stevedores had encountered a problem and wanted one of our crew members to operate the heavy lift crane onboard at the time of discharge of certain heavy cargo. It is irregular for the ship to undertake such work. However, as I have known the capabilities of the Myanmar boatswain and the other two members of the Myanmar crew, I advised him to let one of them handle the heavy lift crane at the time of discharge. I also told him not to forget to ask the receivers for a letter of undertaking or disclaimer in case any damages were incurred to the cargo while being discharged by our crew. I also asked that they be remunerated appropriately for the work. The additional payment had already been discussed and it seemed like only my approval was pending.

As planned, Ibrahim the driver was present to pick me up at 0900 hours. He told me that William was waiting at the office and that he would take me from the agent's office directly to the ship's office. I met with the managing director at the agent's office and had a chat with him over a cup of tea for about fifteen minutes.

Thereafter, together with William, I went in search of Reema's family shop. We got out of the car in front of the shop and walked in. Once inside, we looked around for an employee to ask for Reema's mother. "Can I help you?" asked a girl who came up to me. I appreciated this service very much, and said, "I am here to meet Mrs. Doshi, the owner's wife." While I was talking to her, a young and handsome man walked up to me and asked the same question, "Can I help you?" "Yes, please, I would like to meet with Mrs. Doshi, the owner's wife," I reiterated. "I am the owner's son, Deepak. What can I do for you?" he offered. Despite the flamboyance and gusto, it seemed like he already knew there was a problem in the back of his mind.

I introduced myself. "I am Captain John De Silva and my ship *Eastern Sun* is in port, and this is Mr. William. He is our ship's local agent," I said, as our introductory words. "It seems to me that both of you have not come here to purchase any goods but have something else, something very important to discuss," he analyzed. "You are correct, Deepak," I replied.

He called us into the office. When we stepped inside, I saw a lady who appeared to be his mother poring over some files. Deepak spoke with his mother in their native tongue. I presumed he told the lady that we were there to meet with her. I introduced both myself and William to the lady. "Madam, I am here to discuss a very important matter with you," I said. "I should call my husband. He did not come to the shop with us as he was not feeling well," she responded. "Please do not disturb him now. We will meet with him later," I said accommodatingly. She gave in to my suggestion.

Suddenly, Deepak asked me, "Captain, is it something to do with a nightclub woman whom you met? If that is the case, do not waste your time. She has been cast aside from our family long ago. We are very respectable people. My father is well respected, even by the president of this country. That is why we are continuing our business here or else we have a big business in India, and would have gone back long ago."

This seemed to be getting tougher with Deepak's opening statement. I was glad when he paused. I looked directly at his mother and asked, "Madam, can I tell you my story?" "Yes, yes, please," she said. I was thankful that at least someone here was not into giving heavy introductions.

Deepak did try to break in, but the lady was firm. "This gentleman is a foreigner and has come here specifically to meet with me and your father. If you are not willing to take part in the conversation properly, you may leave this room," she ordered. "Thank you," I said. I explained to her about my meeting with Reema, and related word for word everything Reema had told me – about everything that happened to her after she went with her boyfriend on that fateful day.

It took nearly one hour to complete my story. The lady listened to me intently; time and again, she interrupted to ask some pertinent questions.

"Mrs. Doshi, I, too, have a sister. I love and care for her very much. Reema is your daughter. Please do not let her continue her life of misery and degradation," I appealed to her. Mrs. Doshi was moved to tears.

Deepak stormed in once again and played the villain. "Captain, I do not know why you are so interested in bringing that prostitute back to our family. She is screwing around. She is a bloody whore," he yelled. Mrs. Doshi told him to shut up.

"Would you like to come home and meet with my husband?" she offered. "Most certainly," I said.

At this moment, William received a call from his boss and needed to leave. He took the Doshi's home address and he said that he would be back in about one hour. He asked me to call him if I needed him earlier.

I went to the Doshi's home in our car, and Mrs. Doshi went in their car. On the way, I prayed to God to let me see an end to this girl's suffering. The house was situated in a high-class neighborhood. There were palatial homes everywhere.

Mrs. Doshi's car turned in and we followed her to a house with a large gate, and a security officer at the gate. Once we were parked on the driveway, I told the driver to wait and I got out of the car. Mrs. Doshi signaled for me to come inside.

The house had a large garden. There was a well-maintained front yard with flowers in full bloom. When I walked into the verandah, Mrs. Doshi showed me a seat, which I gladly accepted. It took a few minutes for them to come out, possibly because Mrs. Doshi briefed her husband prior to our meeting. Mr. Doshi was a man of medium build, with a dark complexion He appeared to be in his mid-fifties and had a very stately look.

"I am Doshi. I understand that you are Captain De Silva," he said, extending his hand as he approached me. "Yes, that is right," I responded. He continued, "So, this is about our disdainful daughter? Captain, what is your interest here?" he asked. I explained the whole story to him as lucidly as I could. Time to time I saw his eyebrows moving up and down.

When I was almost through, he began. "Captain, if she was pregnant with an illegitimate child, if she had told her mother we would have helped her. Now the entire family circle and the business circle are aware that she is living in sin. And you know, I had very high hopes for this girl. I loved her very much. Whatever the work, I had I made sure that I took her to school when she was in high school. It was only after she entered college that I let her travel alone and that, too, was in our car. We brought her up like a flower. She was a very sweet girl. She was my whole life. And now, see where she is? She has ruined herself. I just cannot accept her back into our house. What will our servants think?" he asked me.

What their servants thought was the least of my problems. I told him, "We have not come to this world to live here permanently. Our lives are very short. I can see that she is mortally scared of you," I said. "So, is that the reason she ran away with this loser?" he asked me.

I tread very respectfully "Mr. Doshi, can I call her here? I am sure if you meet with her you will understand her better." "Of course, I feel very sad about all that has happened," he said. I waited for a while, and when I looked at him, they were tears in his eyes. I made use of that situation and called her. She immediately answered the phone. "Reema, I will be coming there in a few minutes, please be ready to come back with me," I told her. I could almost hear her breathing. "Can she come with the child," I asked Mrs. Doshi?" "No, not with the child," yelled Mr. Doshi.

As I was getting ready to go, Mrs. Doshi said, "Captain, I will come with you." It was so sudden, but it made me smile, a smile of victory. "You are most welcome," I said.

I gave the address to Ibrahim and it did not take long to reach the place where she lived. Mrs. Doshi waited in the car as she could not climb the stairs to the third floor. I climbed up and my eyes searched for her. As I came up to her floor, I saw Reema standing outside. I realized that she was sharing an apartment with another family. The place was quite crowded. She was very happy to see me and my bodyguard, Ibrahim.

Her first question was, "What did my father say?" "Everything was fine. For the moment, you have to leave the child and come," I said. It seemed as though she had anticipated such a situation and had made arrangements for the child to be taken care of until she returned.

She was well dressed and looked unusually beautiful. She was going home after three years. There was enough reason for her to be happy. As she walked towards the car, her mother got out and extended her arms. What a sight it was! Reema went down on her knees and kissed her mother's feet. There were so many spectators. It was like the making of a film and I was on location, too. They both got into the car and I thanked God. I was very happy.

The time was well past twelve noon. My thoughts were about the ship, too. It was a Sunday yet I did not feel the ease that usually came with the day.

When the car reached Doshi's residence, Mr. Doshi, who had been waiting for the arrival, came out of the house. But he stood straight, possibly trying to hide his emotions. Reema ran up to him, fell at his feet and kissed them; she was asking for his forgiveness. Mr. Doshi could not control his emotions for long. Watching the sight, I had tears streaming down my face as well.

I thanked God— not once, but over and over again.

For about ten to fifteen minutes, there was absolute silence. Nobody spoke. Suddenly, Mrs. Doshi said something to her husband in their mother tongue. Immediately after this whispering, Mr. Doshi invited me to join them for lunch, and I accepted the invitation. I did so mainly because I wanted to assess the situation.

I saw the servants, one after the other; make their way from inside to welcome Reema. Mr. Doshi was happy and after a little while he said, "Captain, I would like to hear something about you and your family." I was happy to answer the question, and opened up to him. Soon, Mr. Doshi was as comfortable with me as I was with him. So, I very quietly asked him, "What are you going to do with Reema?" He said, "She has to stop this nonsense of going to nightclubs. I will give her the money. She ought to find a safe and comfortable place for her and her son to live. I have to deal with my son now, Captain." The worry on his face made him look older. His forehead was creased and his eyes appeared sad. There was a lost look about him. What Reema had told me about her family and their wealth came to my mind. Mr. Doshi said, as if to console himself, "Once I settle matters with my son, I will decide on a long-term plan."

We had a vegetarian lunch. It was tastefully prepared. Reema did not join us at the table. Her absence was nagging at my mind. I was confused. What was the reason she was keeping away from the table at a time when everything seemed to be working out?

I gave Ibrahim some money to have lunch. But it had become his habit to babysit me. He never left me alone.

As I was about to leave, Mr. Doshi asked for my contact details. Thereafter, Mr. and Mrs. Doshi thanked me profusely and repeatedly asked me what I needed. They wanted to know if there was anything they could give me to take away. "Pray for me and my crew as we are going to experience very bad weather. I really don't know what else is in store for us." Mr. Doshi asked how many members were in my crew. "A total of twenty three men," I said. He promised that they would have a religious service for all of us onboard.

To add to the happenings, Reema fell at my feet and began to sob. She would not leave. "Do not thank me; thank God for bringing you back to your family. With God, everything is possible," I told her. I also told her to visit the Reverend Sisters who helped her, and help them in return.

As I was about to leave, Reema, in the presence of her parents, asked for my home address and contact numbers. "Your father has my contact details," I replied. She appeared heartbroken that I did not give her my contact details. I did not want her to remember the sad past. I wanted her to walk into a happy and peaceful future. Mr. Doshi walked up to me just before I was climbing into the car and said, "Captain, I assure you that Reema and her son will be well looked after." "Thank you, and God bless you," I said, linking all my actions with the Divine.

They watched me as I left them. For them, it was a family reunion. For me, it was a pleasant happening on an otherwise dark voyage. The role I played in this real-life drama heartened me to no end. It filled my very being with a deep sense of joy. I had lifted Reema from emotional squalor; I had pulled her parents out of the depths of despair that made them lie sleepless when darkness crept into their hearts.

Chapter Twelve

A Sense of Peace

When I returned to the ship, the chief officer informed me that the cargo work would be completed at approximately 2200 hours. He was keen to know of the sailing plan.

"Brian, it seems there was a problem with remittances that are due to agents. Today is a Sunday so the agents do not have any hopes of receiving it. The payments will be made tomorrow. When the cargo work is over, keep the ship ready for sailing," I said.

I stayed onboard that evening, planning the approach route to the harbor entrance in Mombasa. I thought long and hard about the strong current, known as the East African Coastal Current that sets southwards.

The ship sailed for Mombasa at 1900 hours on June 12, 2006. The distance to Mombasa was about 408 nautical miles. The estimated time of arrival was adjusted to 0600 hours on June 14, 2006.

The weather was more than bad. It was getting ready to give us the hammering of our lives. We were experiencing strong southerly winds of about thirty-five to forty knots and the sea was very rough. While approaching the outer roads of Mombasa, and when the ship was about fifteen nautical miles away from the entrance to the harbor, I called the Mombasa port control on VHF Channel 16.

"Mombasa Port Control, Mombasa Port Control, this is *Eastern Sun.*"

"*Eastern Sun*, you are loud and clear. Shift to Channel 10," responded the Mombasa port control.

The VHF was set to Channel 10. I replied, "Mombasa port control, this is *Eastern Sun*," my ETA pilot boarding grounds, 0600 hours, today. Do you have any instructions for me?"

"*Eastern Sun*, please give the ship's details."

The details asked for were port of registry, flag, call sign, gross registered tonnage, net registered tonnage, official number, International Maritime Organization (IMO) number, cargo onboard, purpose of call, and security level maintained onboard.

"Who is your agent?" asked the controller, after passing and receiving all such details. "Do not have agent's details. Will come back soon with the information," was my reply. I sent a very urgent message to Colombo. The reply went thus: "Agent not appointed as yet. Will revert soon."

I passed the information to port control. Then the person at port control asked, "Captain, I can recommend an agent, if you so desire." I replied, "Affirmative, go ahead with the details." The details of a shipping agent in Mombasa were given to me, and I immediately sent it to Colombo.

"Do not attempt to anchor at the chartered anchorage under present weather conditions. I suggest that you go out and maintain VHF communication range until the agent is appointed and pre-arrival formalities are completed," said the controller thereafter.

The owners, having contacted the agents in Mombasa had appointed them to handle the ship and bunkering. We received berthing instructions at around 1600 hours on June 16, 2006. The ship was moved north and south until then. Soon after receiving berthing instructions, the ship approached the entrance to the Mombasa harbor to pick up the pilot. While approaching, the ship experienced a strong lee drift. However, I managed to maneuver and get the pilot boat alongside and the pilot boarded safely.

I felt a sense of peace engulf me. It was a serenity that set in after such a long time. But alas, the feeling was short-lived.

The ship was moored to mooring buoys in the harbor and the pilot left the ship. A few minutes after the pilot departed, the agent, who had come along with the port authorities, boarded the ship. "Captain, bunkers will only be supplied tomorrow as the full payment for the same is yet to be remitted," said the agent, after introducing himself.

I was happy that I could have a comparatively peaceful night onboard.

The first group of officials we attended, as usual, included the port quarantine officers. The regular set of forms was handed over to them. After receiving the duly completed quarantine forms, the senior of the two officers said, "Captain, could you arrange for one officer to guide us? I want to inspect the ship's galley and provisions rooms." I called the third officer and instructed him to take the officers to the places where they wanted the inspection to be carried out.

I then attended to the customs and immigration formalities, and both officers had no queries but awaited the quarantine officer's clearance.

The third officer, who went with the quarantine officer, arrived and informed me that they wished to speak with me. "Captain, are you breeding cockroaches on this ship? There are thousands of them in the galley where your food is being kept, and in the provisions rooms, too. I am unable to grant quarantine clearance under such circumstances," he said.

After having made this frightening proclamation, he wanted to talk with me in private and wanted me to take them to my cabin. All others, including the agent, were sitting in the officers' smoke room.

I ushered the two officers into my office. They came straight to the point. "Captain, are you ready to discuss with us so that we can give you the certificate and leave?" "What is it you want to discuss?" I asked, expecting an answer. I had sailed too long, dealt with officers like these gentlemen for too long, to not know what they were talking about.

"You know, Captain, if I detain the ship your owners will have to fumigate the ship. Then, your agent would have to arrange for one of the companies here in Mombasa to carry out this task. As you are already aware, it cannot be done when you and your crew are onboard. Therefore, after preparing the ship for fumigation, all of you must leave to a hotel, ashore, and may have to stay there for about twenty-four to thirty-six hours. That is the minimum time period. The sailing of the ship will be delayed and it will incur additional port charges. Accordingly to my total estimate, it will come to about USD 10,000. This excludes the loss of time on the voyage," he explained gravely. "Considering what you have to pay otherwise, I think USD 2,000 will be a very reasonable amount," he said, and I almost held onto my chair. I did not have USD 2,000 to pay them.

I was in trouble once again. God help me!

I called the agent and asked him if he could negotiate with them and bring about a settlement. The agent did not want to get involved. So, I was left to handle the matter alone. At that time all that remained of the ship's cash was about USD 400. On earlier occasions, some of the Myanmar officers had money and I borrowed from them. In the present situation, the majority of the crew was very new and they did not have any money.

I used the agent's mobile phone and called the MD. When he came on the line, I explained the situation. On hearing my story, he became hysterical, and began to scream. "John, what the hell is going on? We have problems in every damn port your ship goes to. Why don't you throw in some money and get the matter sorted out?" I said "Shaun, if you go through my messages to you and the operations manager, you will see how many of them I have sent you since April, informing you about the cockroach menace onboard. Here, we are in hell already. I only have about USD 400 with me. I will give the phone to the agent— you speak with him and try to get some money."

In the meantime, the customs and immigration officers had finished their part of the work and wanted to leave. When I got the message, I came down and thanked them, and handed over their handouts, and they left.

Thereafter, the agent spoke with Shaun Gomes. After finishing the conversation, the agent asked me who that was. I told him that he was the MD of the management company of the ship. "Captain, what the hell does he think of us? This man hollered at me, and was disparaging. He sends a ship infested with cockroaches and blames me for not handling the quarantine officers properly. I am going to inform my boss."

Then the agent, who was a young lad, asked me "Captain, how do you live on this ship?" I went into the chief engineer's cabin, and it was full of cockroaches. It is not fair to treat the crew in this way.

The agent spoke with his boss and at the end of the conversation, gave the phone to me. Mr. Amir, his boss said, "Captain, welcome to Mombasa. Thank you for getting us the business. With regard to the quarantine, I will handle it. But, after hearing what my colleague had to say about the presence of cockroaches onboard, I very sincerely suggest you consider the sicknesses that you and your crew may suffer later on due to cockroach bites and cockroaches getting into your food. You should ensure that this menace is eliminated before the ship sails from Mombasa. It is not the money, Captain. I feel for the human beings onboard. After all, all of you are there to earn something for the family. Not to fall sick because of some defiant action and the indifference of your owner with regard to this matter. I will call the ship's management right away and emphasize that they must immediately approve the fumigation. Further delays will attract the attention of the PSC Officer and if he boards, the ship will surely be detained," explained Mr. Amir.

A little while later, Shaun Gomes called me on the agent's phone. Before he could say anything, I asked him "What is it now? Do you think your bloody ship is the QE-2?" "John, please listen to me. You know our financial position is bad. We need time to borrow some money and transfer it. Our next cargo is ready and the charterer is putting a lot of pressure on us. Therefore, in order to save time, please give the agent an assurance on my behalf, and kindly ask them to arrange for the fumigation, removal of crew, and soon after, the crew returns onboard, a supply of bunkers," he pleaded.

After listening to him, I said," I will try to persuade them." Then he suggested to me that I should get the agent to get me a local mobile phone or card for the ship's mobile phone, so he could call me directly.

In the meantime, the quarantine officers had a discussion with the agent, collected their handouts, and left.

I was very happy, in a way, because all of us onboard had been suffering badly due to the cockroaches.

Chapter Thirteen

Away with Roaches and Rats

At around 1200 hours on June 17, 2006, the agent came onboard with the representative of the company assigned to carry out the fumigation and also the ship chandler. I instructed the person from the fumigation company to carry out a comprehensive fumigation taking into consideration the possibility of the presence of rats onboard. After having experienced a myriad of problems due to the complacency and indifference of the management, I did not want to lose the opportunity to get things done properly.

I instructed the second officer to deal with the ship chandler who had been appointed to remove the provisions from the ship and store them in their storeroom and supply other fresh provisions that we would order. In the meantime, the chief officer took care of preparing the ship for fumigation.

The agent informed me that Shaun Gomes had advised him to find a cheap hotel to put all officers and crew, and to check them out of the hotel at 12 noon tomorrow regardless of whether the vessel was ready or not. However, he wanted me to check into a "good hotel." I detested such an attitude. After listening to what the agent had to tell me, I told him to take me to the hotel he had selected for my crew. We got into the waiting boat and proceeded ashore.

When we stepped ashore, the agent took me to a guest house where he had planned to house my officers and crew. I did not like the place. I went in with him and inspected one room. I found that the room was very dirty, the toilet was in a dilapidated state, the beds were broken, and the bed sheets were torn and dirty.

After my inspection, I asked the agent, "How much for the room?" He said, "Captain, as we were talking about eleven rooms, the rate was set at USD 40 just for the room." The agent's name was Frank. "Frank, from what I observe, this seems to be a place where people bring prostitutes and spend a very short time. I strongly feel that it is not fair to put my crew up in this place. Please take me to a better place and let me decide. I guarantee you the payments," I told Frank. Frank responded with a smile. "Captain, I am extremely sorry, I was only following the instructions of your company's managing director. You know that he is a very hot tempered man. A slight provocation will set him off." "Leave that part to me," I said.

I was taken to another hotel, and when we got there I spoke with the front office manager. As we were making a bulk reservation, he agreed to sell a room for USD 45, given that it was on a half-board basis, at USD 60 per double room.

However, it seemed that Frank was not too happy that I had intervened and personally dealt with this matter. When I sensed his disappointment and the dark cloud over his enthusiasm, I told him, "Frank, when you are preparing the disbursement procedure, please add ten percent because the payment will be done by your company." "Captain, we have to add twenty percent because of the other expenses involved," he responded happily. "Okay, the front office manager will offer you a commission. I do not know who will take it. If you want to collect it, please do. But, in this case do not add more than ten percent," I said, and he agreed.

Three persons from a private security company were employed to keep a watch on the ship.

Thereafter, the entire crew was taken to the hotel. Prior to leaving the ship, I addressed all my officers and crew and told them that the night was all theirs, but that they must be very careful when going into nightclubs and other such places. I emphasized the fact that this was a Godsend opportunity for all of us for we had suffered severely due to the cockroach menace. I was fortunate enough to have a disciplined crew. I remembered the precious members of the crew from Myanmar and their sense of discipline. I had to appreciate them all.

We moved into the hotel at around 1900 hours on June 18, 2006. I had a call from Akram immediately after I checked in. He was the chief of the company that was carrying out the fumigation. "Captain, I understand that you and your crew checked into the hotel. I am calling to invite you and the chief engineer to dinner," he said. "Thank you," I responded and said, "I have my chief officer here with us. I would like to bring him along, too." "He is most welcome," said Akram.

The three of us met Akram at the lobby of the hotel at 2030 hours. "Captain, what kind of food would you like to have? Just give me an idea of how you would like to spend the evening. I am asking all these questions because I want you to have a nice evening," he said, in all cordiality.

"Besides the food, I would like to go to a place where there is live music. When I say music, I mean country and western stuff!" I said lightly. "There is a beach resort north of the city, called Serena Beach Hotel. Let us go there," he said, after some thought.

While being driven to the Serena Beach Resort, I pondered over the grueling situations that I had been going through. With the grace of God, I had endured the toughest of them all and come out unscathed, I thought to myself. My trust in God was firm and unwavering. And it was God who was with me on these moments of varying dangers, threats, and uncertainty.

I knew that God himself had presented me with this opportunity— not merely to safeguard our health but to pull us out of the monotony and uncertainty onboard. This was indeed a God-given opportunity, no doubt. After about twenty minutes of driving, we turned into Serena Beach Hotel. It was a Thursday, and there was an impressive crowd. There were a greater number of foreigners. I took an immediate liking to the place.

We were taken directly to the main restaurant and bar area. There was a three-piece band getting ready to perform. It had been a long time since I was this happy. I made my way to the washroom. On my way back, I met a member of the band. I introduced myself and asked him where he was from. He said that the three of them were from the Philippines, and that they had a contract with the management of the hotel. He said that they also performed in another hotel which was under the same management. Filipinos were talented musicians. There was a carefree, lighthearted happiness in the air. Everything was set for the evening.

The bandleader came up to our table and wanted me to request some songs. I immediately gestured to a steward for a note paper and wrote down ten songs. The band played all the songs that I requested in the first session.

It is customary to tip when a wonderful job has been done. I was generous with the tipping because I was very happy. It was an unforgettable evening. The only sobering factor was that Akram was a non-drinker. However, he kept us company with copious quantities of soda. We finished our dinner and left the hotel at about 0030 hours.

The fumigation was carried-out on the morning of June 19, 2006. On the following day, at around 1200 noon, the agent called me "Captain, the company that carried out the fumigation is advising me not to send the crew back to the ship until tomorrow morning, due to the presence of toxic gases," he said. "In that case, please arrange with the hotel for us to stay for one more night," I responded. He said he would arrange for this extension.

I called the MD and updated him on the current situation. He, as usual, was only interested in getting the ship out as soon as possible. I asked him whether he could arrange for some money to pay cash advances to officers and crew. "John, here we are struggling to pay up agency fees, port dues, and bunker charges, and you want your crew to have a holiday?" he almost yelled. His attitude did not come as a surprise. Shaun had obviously never won any medals for being nice and polite.

"Shaun, you must understand that all the problems I have faced so far on this ship were due to your shortcomings— your negativity, arrogance, and your inability to think of the crew as human beings and not parts of the machinery. It seems as though you have still not learned a lesson. I am reluctantly compelled to say that you are a lousy ship manager. I ask God to help you change your attitude." There was no sound from the other end. Then came a quiet voice. "I am sorry, John; the company does not have any money. The previous charterer has deducted all the losses incurred during the ship's stay in Lobito, and for the delayed delivery of cargo and spoiled cargo. Anyway, about how many US dollars do you need?" "If possible, around USD 1,500, to pay the crew a small cash advance," I said. "It will be arranged. John, I know you are very annoyed with me. Do not think I am not aware of what you have done and every step you have taken to keep the ship in operation during the past few months. I do not need anyone's reports. You are my friend, and I depend on you. Sorry about all that has happened. When you come home, we will go out for a drink and you can pour your heart out to me then. Until then, please bear with all the shortcomings," he consoled.

I had nothing to say. In fact, I was looking forward to expressing the exasperation that I felt. The problems that I had encountered and the responsibility of my crew among other factors, and the spurts of violent irregularities were far too vast to wait to be discussed over the promised drink. That was the end of the conversation.

About one hour later, the agent called and said that he was not able to get the US dollars because of the short notice, but that it could be paid in local currency. I consulted the crew, and they were ready to accept the advance in local currency. The advance was paid in Kenyan Shillings and was equivalent to about USD 1,200.

The members of the crew who received cash left the hotel immediately. I stayed in the hotel that evening and spent it with the few who remained. In the meantime, I advised the chief officer to prepare the ship for sailing as soon as we returned tomorrow. It was an early and peaceful night for us.

The next morning, as I was getting ready to go down and join the others for breakfast, I heard a knock on the door. When I opened the door, I found the chief officer with the agent. The agent had arrived to inform me that one of the crew who went out last night had been admitted to a hospital as he had been robbed and assaulted mercilessly. I, along with the chief officer went to the hospital where my crew member had been admitted.

On speaking with him, I learned that he had met a girl in a nightclub and had gone with her to her house. Some men stormed in during the night and he fought with them as they were trying to rob him. He stated that he had lost all his money, his wristwatch, and a gold ring. The girl had called police, who then brought him to the hospital and had informed the agent.

Fortunately, his injuries were not life-threatening. The matron of the ward informed us that the crew member could be discharged after the senior medical officer of the ward examined him at 9:00 a.m.

As the agent was ready to check the crew out of the hotel and return them to the ship, I sent the chief officer with him and stayed back to meet with the ward doctor. Precisely at 9:00 a.m., the doctor came on his rounds and the matron was kind enough to bring the doctor to see my crew member first.

The doctor read the report that hung on the bed head and thereafter told Anthony, my crew member, to get down from the bed and walk a few feet. Then he asked him to get back in bed, and asked the matron to cover the bed with a screen for a further examination.

After examining the patient, the doctor called me in and told me that it was necessary to take an X-ray of the skull and the right collar bone. He went on to say that it would be better if Anthony was taken to a private hospital for the X-ray and for faster results.

I called the agent and told him what had to be done. A car was sent from the agent's office with a young man to guide us. X-rays were taken and we returned to the hospital within an hour and a half.

We were taken to the consultant with the X-ray reports. As he was a visiting consultant specialist, we had to pay a consultation fee. After inspecting the reports and examining the patient, the doctor prescribed some painkillers and advised him to be discharged. I thanked God.

Anthony did not want any of the medical expenses to be forwarded to the company. He said he would pay his own bills. I appreciated that very much, and I shared in the payment of his bills. The chief officer and the chief engineer were also kind enough to pay a share of the expenses.

By 1700 hours on June 20, 2006, the ship was ready, per the owners' instructions, to sail for Salalah, a port in the southern part of Oman. The sky was overcast with patches of threatening clouds. The wind was strong, at times gusting to about 40 to 45 knots. The sea was rough. I sensed that the start of the voyage was a prelude to what we were about to experience. I stood alone on the starboard wing of the bridge. While watching the ship move ahead, I pondered the events that took place during the ship's stay at the ports of Dar es Salaam and Mombasa. Reema's grueling story came to my mind; despair had turned into hope, and her brother's hostile tentacles had lost their grip.

God was kind and loving. He was able to solve the most complex of our problems. The amazing transformation of Reema's father, those melting moments with her mother, and the complete change brought into Reema's previous lifestyle; a change which she, knowing her parents so well, thought was impossible, the end of the cockroach menace and the threat of ill health; the saving of our crew members from bodily damage at the hands of robbers; these were all acts of the Divine in which I played the role of a middleman in prayer.

The drama seemed to be over and the sea lay ahead. The waves beckoned and I had to tear myself away from the feelings. This is the life of a seafarer. The land is but a temporary haven in which relationships are made and the "blue sea" is the place where memories are relieved and silent teardrops join the mighty ocean.

The voyage was planned while taking into consideration the presence of pirates around the Somali coast. The route was initially set to be on an easterly course to a position about 250 nautical miles northwest of Seychelles, and thereafter maintain a distance of about 400 nautical miles off the Somali coast and proceed north.

The first night was very peaceful because there was no customary rustling of cockroaches. According to reports, the weather around Socotra, a large island located between the Guardafui Channel and the Arabian Sea, was bad. If it was bad now, the question was how bad would it be when we finally got to the area!

Except for the uncertainty of pirates and our distress due to the prevailing weather conditions, everything else onboard seemed okay.

On the fourth day at sea, the ship started to roll heavily at times due to the sea and swell. Certain adjustments were made from time to time, but the conditions had to be endured. The weather deteriorated further when the ship was about 300 nautical miles from the destination. The morale of the crew onboard was low; I observed them being torn asunder – spending time only to discuss the day-to-day affairs. They appeared to be despairing, and I visited them frequently and spoke with them to provide confidence and engage them in conversation. In order to prevent any more misery from settling into their minds, I got them involved in doing some work in the living area. Whoever could cook was given an opportunity to try his hand in the culinary arts. This kept their minds occupied.

It was not possible to proceed to the designated port. I had a discussion with the chief engineer and chief officer. The chief engineer confirmed that the ship could reach Fujairah, a port in the United Arab Emirates (UAE), situated on the Gulf of Oman. I familiarized the managers with the circumstances and requested permission to divert to Fujairah. The diversion was approved, and we changed course immediately.

As soon as the course was altered, rolling reduced and it was very comfortable after about five days. I maintained my position with regard to relinquishing command of the ship. It seemed that the plan to offer the ship for inspection to the prospective charterers had been postponed. The owners wanted the ship repaired prior to inspection.

On June 26, 2006, at around 1000 hours, the ship entered the Gulf of Oman, sheltered waters from the southwest monsoon weather. Once the ship was in calm conditions, it was decided that we stop and drift in order to make urgent repairs to the auxiliary and main engines. There was no way we could have stopped earlier, even for five minutes, due to the inclement weather.

We resumed our voyage after drifting for about twelve hours. It was heartening to see the ship's crew back at work and engaged in an active lifestyle. The ship arrived at Fujairah anchorage at around 0700 hours on June 29, 2006. It took a while for the port to accept the ship as an "arrived ship", as it was not a planned call.

However, the agents for the ship had been appointed. Due to their able handling of affairs, the port informed me that the ship could receive bunkers and replenish stores about five hours after arrival. From the correspondence between the owners and the agents, it appeared that after bunkering, we had to wait there until a port was found to carry out repairs.

On June 29, 2006, at around 1800 hours, the agent advised that they were having discussions with the port manager of Ras al-Khaimah in the UAE, to get the ship to that destination for repairs.

This was good news for us onboard. On the following day, I received instructions from the managers to proceed to Ras al-Khaimah and anchor at the outer roads. When the instructions were received, we sailed from Fujairah at around

2000 hours and proceeded to Ras al-Khaimah. It was a short passage and the ship reached the destination in approximately twelve hours with adjusted speed. After anchoring close to the fairway buoy at around 0530 hours on July 1, 2006, I called the agent on my mobile phone. He told me that a launch would arrive at 0700 hours on the morning of July 2, and advised me to be present for a meeting at the port manager's office.

In the meantime, my chief officer and I studied the topography of the port, the approach, and adjacent sea coast together. We found that the port was uncharted, meaning no approach had been marked on the charts. This was a very bad situation for me as the captain. The responsibility lay heavily on my shoulders. We also learned that no port in the Persian Gulf, other than this one, was prepared to give a long-term berth for repairs. Trying times lay ahead.

Again, I prayed to God to give me the wisdom to make the right decision.

The launch was alongside the ship on July 2, 2006, at 0730 hours. I went ashore with the second officer of the ship. The second officer is also the navigator. I observed the approach route to the port while traveling in the boat. There was no marked channel so I requested the coxswain of the boat to go to a point approximately one nautical mile from the entrance to the port and resume the approach. In this way, I was able to observe a few conspicuous shore objects, such as high rise buildings, in line with the entrance to the port. I found four strong landmarks to assist with our approach. The entrance was well marked with two pillars. I did not remember whether they had lights on them or not. It was a day approach, however, and the question of lights would not matter.

After forty-five minutes, the launch reached a newly constructed pier. It appeared sturdy and was obviously for passenger traffic. The agent was already there when I reached the port manager's office. The manager was a hydrographer by profession. He had all the plans of the port as well as water and depth soundings. But he did not have any acceptable information on the approach route. What he had was two or three lines of depth soundings.

I was not satisfied with this sparse information. However, I needed to assess the situation and include all available data. In order to make a decision of whether or not to bring the ship– I had to weigh the pros and cons. The agent was somewhat forceful, and was directly pressuring me to accept the manager's offer and bring the ship in without delay. Thus, we boarded the port launch and proceeded towards the entrance. I suggested that we proceed out so that I could enlighten the manager where I wanted the depth soundings. They agreed to my request.

We proceeded about one nautical mile to the route we used when coming in by the launch boat. I showed the manager the conspicuous objects I would be using as guidelines to take the depth soundings. It would be necessary for me to bring the ship into port and berth alongside without additional assistance. No pilots or tugs would be in attendance. All these factors had to be taken into consideration when charting the correct course.

We spent almost the entire day in port and returned to the ship around 1700 hours. By the time we returned, I was running a fever. This came as no surprise. The stress I was experiencing, along with the worry and uncertainty of our course, was as wide as the sea itself. I had a long discussion with the chief officer, chief engineer and second officer upon returning to the ship. I was fully aware, however, that not only was the decision ultimately mine, but the responsibility was, too. If I tried to take the ship in and experienced problems such as grounding, I would be in deep trouble. Furthermore, if any damage to the bottom of the ship caused an oil leak, I could end up in an Arabian jail.

If I decided not to go in, there was a chance that the port manager would change his mind and the owners might have to bring the ship all the way back to Colombo. The ship was not in the proper condition to take up a voyage of that nature and it did not have sufficient bunkers to support the trip. The issues with that alternative choice seemed far heavier than the decision to navigate the unchartered waters within the port.

I received several telephone calls in the meantime from the MD and the agents. They had apparently spoken to each other prior to calling me. "John, I understand that there is no problem and that you can take the ship in and berth," was the MD's opening line; the usual assumption of the best under the worst of situations. "Shaun, do you know that the port is still not chartered and it has no marked approach channel?" I asked him. "I can arrange a pilot," he offered graciously. I asked him, "From where?" "You must have seen some small ships inside the port transporting cement or some such items. Those captains are very experienced and they will help you take the ship in," Shaun replied.

I did not like what he was getting at. "Yes, not only have I seen those ships, I have also visited two and met with their captains. They are very small ships. The length of each was about 160 to 170 feet with a draft under loaded conditions of about 10 to 11 feet," I said.

"Those captains, they are Arabs. In my opinion, they did it by experience, and they have nothing to lose if anything goes wrong. Have you forgotten that our ship is 485 feet long and, at present, in ballast condition has a maximum draught of about 18 feet? Please talk sense, and refrain from talking nonsense. I expect a person of your caliber to talk like a professional. That is something you have not been doing during the past six months," I said. After listening to me he said, "John, this is my last request. I am making arrangements to relieve you soon. I am also waiting to come there to arrange repairs." "If everything goes well, I will be relieved. If something goes wrong, I will end up in an Arab jail for the rest of my life. You think, after having gone through everything these past few months, I will take such a chance for your sake?" I questioned. "John, I leave the decision with you. Good luck," he said, without fanfare.

Thereafter, the agent called me and I asked for three hours to make a decision.

After our discussion I went into my cabin, showered, and prayed. I went down on my knees and prayed to God to give me the wisdom to do his will.

I called the MD at around 0800 hours on July 3, 2006, and told him to arrange two tugs. I said I would take the ship in on the morning of July 4, just after sunrise. He communicated my decision to the agents and two tugs were arranged.

The agents said that two pilots were also arranged. I inquired, "The port manager said there were no pilots in this port. You were aware of that. From where did you find two pilots now? Who are they?" I asked. He then admitted that they were the captains from the ships we had visited in the port and that their charges were USD 1,000 each. I told him that it did not come as a surprise to me as this was how our MD worked, and that I did not take his actions very seriously anymore. "I will be bringing my ship in, and I will take the full responsibility," I said. The agent sounded relieved, as did the MD. As for me, I felt my creator working within me.

I had informed my wife earlier about the unusual exercise that might take place. I called her and said, "I am going to do it tomorrow at daybreak." She said, "I am very proud of you, and so are the children. We are praying, and everything will be good." I replied, "Thanks, I will call you when I am at berth."

Each crew member was aware of the exercise and I was confident that we could do it. At 0600 hours on July 4, 2006, the agent informed me that the tugs were ready and on standby at the port entrance. It was a clear day. There was not much wind. Visibility was very good. It was high tide at the time. What else do you need, I thought? God is on the job!

Both tug masters were Indians, and the problem of communication was resolved by the use of English. Everybody on the ship was on standby at their respective positions: the chief officer was at the forecastle deck (bow), in charge of forward stations, with the boatswain and other crew. The third officer was on the bridge with me. The second officer was in charge of the after stations with his crew.

I prayed first. Thereafter, I instructed the main engines to be on standby. As soon as the engine room responded, at around 0630 hours, I instructed the chief officer to start heaving the anchor. The anchor was heaved under power.

At 0650 hours, the chief officer reported anchor weight, meaning the anchor was above the water.

At 0655 hours, the engines were placed on dead slow ahead. The speed was about four knots. The ship turned around and we set course on about 090 deg. The depth sounder was continuously monitored. The ship moved ahead almost parallel to the coastline, maintaining a distance of about three miles.

The distance from the anchor position to the position where I had set course to enter port was about two nautical miles. The ship maintained minimum speed up to that position. So far, under keel clearance recorded, the distance between the ship's bottom and the seabed was noted by the depth sounder to be roughly 11 feet, 06 inches. We were doing well.

The ship arrived at the designated position around 0720 hours. *Eastern Sun* was stopped and the engines were reversed to break the headway. Instructions to the tugs were given in the following words.

I called "Tug 1, Tug 1. This is *Eastern Sun*." Tug 1 replied, "Yes, this is Tug 1." I said, "Good morning, Master. Make fast on the starboard bow. Ship's line – the line is given from the ship. Be ready for push, and pull. Once connected, keep the line slack all the time, until further instructions." Tug 1 replied, "Good morning, Captain. Instructions well understood."

Thereafter, I called forward stations, and instructed the chief officer, "Make fast Tug 1 on the Starboard bow. And keep both anchors standby to use in an emergency. If used, short scope only. Just to break headway and stop the ship." The chief officer confirmed that the message was well understood.

I called, "Tug 2, Tug 2. This is *Eastern Sun*." Tug 2 replied, "*Eastern Sun*, this is Tug 2." I said, "Good morning, Master. Make fast right astern. Take the ship's line and keep a long length. Once made fast, watch the propeller. Make sure the line is clear of the propeller at all times. And wait for further instructions." Tug 2 replied, "Good morning, Captain. Instructions well noted."

At around 0745 hours, maneuvering resumed. The ship was swung around to approach the port entrance, keeping two tall and conspicuous buildings as the direction line

My instruction to the helmsman, as I gave him the course to steer, was to keep the ship to the middle of the entrance to the port. I also advised him to not get panicked. He needed to keep his eyes wide open, and be fully focused on the job.

To the third officer, who was with me on the bridge, I asked him to monitor the ship's position frequently, and keep watch on the depth sounder and helmsman.

The order to the engine room was, "Okay let's start. Dead slow ahead."

When I called the engine room, the chief engineer answered. "Good Morning, Chief. The drama just started." "Good luck and God bless, Captain, see you in Ras al-Khaimah," he replied.

We commenced approach at around 0755 hours and the ship entered the harbor at around 0820 hours. The tugs were instructed as follows: "Tug 1, get closer to the starboard bow, and lean on. Just lean on. Do not push." "Tug 2, slowly stretch the line. Repeat, only stretch the line.

So far, the minimum depth recorded was about five feet. The ship was going to be berthed portside to the berth.

At 0825 hours, the engine was stopped when the bow was in line with the western end of the pier. I allowed the headway to take her. Once the ship was well in line and off the berth, I ordered dead slow astern. Then, I said, "Tug 1, standby to push." "Tug 2, come round on the starboard side and push easy." "Tug 1, push very easy." "Tug 2, push me very easy." Tug 1 replied. "Pushing easy, Sir." Tug 2 replied, "As you said, Sir."

Both tugs started pushing the ship towards the berth. When the distance between the port side of the ship and the pier was about 100 feet, I said, "Tug 1, stop pushing." "Tug 2, stop pushing and break up -- move away."

With those orders, the ship moved gently towards the berth. Mooring lines were passed and one head movement by the engine was required to bring her to the proper position.

Both tug masters did a wonderful job. It was a well-controlled maneuver, and the ship was berthed at around 0845 hours on July 4, 2006.

I called both tugs. "Tug 1, this is *Eastern Sun*." Tug 1 replied, "*Eastern Sun*, this is Tug 1." I said, "Thank you, Master. That was a good job. Have a great day." The response from Tug 1 was, "You are welcome, Captain. You, too, have a great day."

"Tug 2, this is *Eastern Sun*." Reply from the tug, "*Eastern Sun*, this Tug 2." "Thank you, Master, for the good job. Have a great day." Reply came back as, "Captain, you are welcome, see you at sailing time."

The tugs were cast off. I rushed into my bedroom, prayed, and thanked God for bringing us in safely. Glory be to God! God is great all the time!

An hour or so later, the agent and the port manager boarded the ship and congratulated me. "All should go to my Lord and my God. It is with his grace everything is done," I said.

I had a message from MD that he would be arriving the next day. We were safe in a beautiful port. It was summer, the hot season in the gulf, and the temperature inside the ship rose to about 45 degrees to 50 degrees Celsius between 1200 and 1600 hours. As the air-conditioning system on the ship had broken down, we had no other alternative than to bear the scorching heat.

The MD arrived in Ras al-Khaimah at around 0900 hours on July 5, 2006. I called a meeting which was attended by the chief officer and chief engineer. The main topics were the repair of the ship's generators, the air-conditioning system, and the repairs to be carried out to eliminate a long list of shortcomings on the mechanical side as noted by the surveyor at Douala. The discussion also featured key issues like a cash advance for crew, the assistant cook not wanting to continue working onboard, and the purchase of provisions as there was an immediate need for replenishment. Word had come in that monthly allotments had also not been received by the next-of-kin of many crew members.

It is true that I have referred to Shaun Gomes, the MD of the ship's management company, as my friend. But sadly I felt so let down. I had done so much for him. I had endured a great deal for our friendship's sake. I was on the path of the Lord, and I have learned to love all, even those who have disappointed me such as Shaun Gomes.

The MD boarded the ship at around 1600 hours. After some initial small talk, and with his permission, I called the chief officer and the chief engineer. They had met the MD prior to leaving Colombo to board the ship. This, however, was under different circumstances. I let the chief engineer open the discussion with matters concerning machinery which needed urgent repairs.

In the meantime, the steward brought in tea. The MD did not seem to like his attire and interrupted the discussion. He said, "John, discipline on the ship is poor. What is this man wearing?" The steward was wearing breeches and a short-sleeved shirt. I said, "Shaun, now that you have asked me a question, I want to give you a detailed answer." I told the chief officer and the chief engineer to excuse us for a few minutes.

"Shaun, discipline on all the ship's that I have commanded so far has been good. You know that better than anyone else. Before focusing on the steward's attire, I would like to remind you of when the previous second engineer tried to assault the chief engineer, and once tried to kill him. I informed you, and pleaded with you to remove him from the ship. Did you do that? No. I knew you could not find a replacement because nobody wanted to join your ship and you did not want to spend money on his repatriation and the airfare of the relief," I poured out to him.

"There would have been mutiny onboard, on several occasions, because of this officer. He was also found to be very incompetent. I informed you, what else could I do? What action did you take? None, none whatsoever. No action was taken. Now let me explain about this steward," I said. I called in the steward, and when he came back, I said, "This man has never worked on a ship before. He joined together with the others in Cape Town. He was seasick from the time the ship left the port and did not do any work for the first few days onboard. I had to get a deck boy to cover his work. Once, when I asked him if he had any prior training to work as a steward on a ship, he said he had worked in a small restaurant as a galley boy. However, he applied for a few jobs, and your company accepted him on the condition that he paid his return airfare in advance. So, he paid your company about USD 900 to get this job. He did not know the work, he had a bad attitude, and he was dangerous, too. The chief officer did not want to deal with him and said that if I pushed him to work, there was a good chance that this man might take a knife and stab me."

"I know that you are now fiercely drafting your answer, but these are the facts onboard," I said with certainty. "Why didn't you inform us?" he asked. "It would have had the same effect as the situation with the former second engineer. I did not want to waste any time. I just want to get the hell off of this ship, Mr. MD," I said.

Having listened to my statement carefully, he remained quiet for a short while. Then, with a sudden outburst, he reprimanded the steward, and told him that he would be sent home soon. However, it did not happen, at least not to my knowledge! The chief officer and chief engineer were called back in to join the meeting. The steward was excused and, prior to leaving the cabin, apologized to us.

I was aware that the steward had only one pair of black trousers and two white short-sleeved shirts. The company did not pay a uniform allowance, and uniforms were not compulsory in the company. Therefore, the MD could not expect the steward to appear in a uniform. Nevertheless, in order to maintain standards, I suggested to the steward that he should wear a uniform when serving meals in the mess room. He very humbly told me that he did not have any other white shirts. The chief officer and I each gave him a white shirt. When he boarded the ship, he did not know the basics about the work of a steward. However, again, the chief officer and I tried our best to instill capabilities which made his work rise to acceptable standards.

After the steward left, the MD poured more tea, and got back into his seat.

"John, when do you want to leave?" he asked gallantly. I chuckled. Was it happiness? Was it disbelief? Or was it sarcasm that I heard in my laughter? "Immediately, Shaun – immediately," I burst out. He took a little time to think and said, "Can I ask you a favor? Today is July 5. Can I arrange your relief around July 11? By that time, I presume much of the repair will be over."

I did not mind staying another week or so for the sake of my crew. But I did not want to show him any great enthusiasm.

"Yes, that will be fine," I said. He was chipper and invited me to go with him to his hotel for drinks and dinner. I did not have a shore leave pass at that time. Anyway, I was in no mood to sit with him for drinks.

I asked God's forgiveness for my display of arrogance. But I was only human and these circumstances were more than trying. A few minutes later, he called a taxi and assured me that he would be back by 0700 hours the following day. I sat alone in my cabin and pondered the events of the recent past. Suddenly, it struck like a thunderbolt that when I was praying one day I did get a message from God that I would be leaving the ship in forty-four days. I got the message on June 10. Therefore, forty-four days counted down to July 24. It was God's message and I was ready to endure any situation until that time. However, I kept this all to myself.

I called home and my daughter answered the phone, "Hi Dad, when are you coming home?" "Very soon, very soon," I replied. "What, tomorrow?" she asked. She was excited. "No, not tomorrow. In about a week," was my quick response. Then my wife came on the line." I heard something like you are coming home soon!" "Yes, in about a week. Everything went on well on berthing the ship in Ras al-Khaimah." She said, "Praise the Lord. I am happy that you are being relieved. But I shall pray hard for the guy, whoever it is, who is coming to relieve you that he will not go through what you have faced so far." I told her, "I do not know, at this moment, who will be relieving me. But I am sure of one thing. No Sri Lankan master would come. But that is Shaun's problem."

"Was it really necessary to go through all that misery? I am sorry to say that. After hearing your friend's way of doing things, I keep my fingers crossed, of course. I pray that you will be relieved soon," she said very softly.

The rest of the evening was peaceful.

Chapter Fourteen

Wanting to Break Free

A t around 0630 hours on July 6, 2006, the chief officer met with me and said that the cook wanted to speak to me. I called the cook and told him to meet me after serving breakfast. I said that the chief officer also ought to be present. However, it completely slipped my mind that the MD would be onboard by that time, and possibly having breakfast with us.

As expected, the MD walked into my cabin just after 0700 hours. "Shaun, would you like to have some tea first, or do we go down for breakfast?" I asked. "Let's go for breakfast," he replied. The three of us went down to the mess room. The steward was in his proper attire, a pair of black trousers and a white short-sleeved shirt, clean and well-ironed. It was a pleasant and formal atmosphere we experienced first thing that morning.

The chief engineer also joined us at breakfast. Our discussion resumed at the breakfast table.

The MD indicated that the owners had decided to make the ship mechanically sound and safe, and also to have clean trading certificates. It sounded very encouraging, at least for the crew who were onboard and had experienced the current shortcomings of the ship. There was always a certain amount of doubt over the statements made by the MD, perhaps due to his questionable actions of the past.

July was possibly the hottest month in the Persian Gulf. The heat was unbearable. The crew wandered around the deck at night, often until about one or two o'clock each morning, because it was too hot to even walk into their cabins before that time. Some of them suffered from skin rashes. Fortunately, we had a good agent. He did his best to arrange medical treatment for the afflicted members of the crew.

The cook refused to work and wanted to sign off and proceed home. He gave an ultimatum that he would only cook dinner up until the day that the ship arrived in port. I had to make arrangements for breakfast the following day to feed the crew. I was happy, in a way, that the MD was there to witness all these happenings. The cook, too, had come on the same terms as the steward.

The breakfast was somehow managed, with two crew members coming to the rescue. I had to arrange with our regular ship chandler, however, to supply three meals, as per our order. The cook was idling until he was sent home a few days later at his own expense.

I learned some inside information, from the boatswain, about the cook who left the ship: He had joined the vessel as someone in Colombo had told him the ship was bound for a port in North America. It appears that the man's ultimate aim had been to jump-ship on arrival at the designated American port. After he realized this ship would never go to that side of the world, he had not wanted to continue, especially under the present circumstances. In short, he had joined the ship to take a free ride to America. Poor man; unfortunately, he got on the wrong ship.

The MD was busy the next few days with representatives from various workshops and their quotes offered for repairs onboard. It took a while for him to decide and distribute the work between three ship-repair workshops in Dubai. The actual repairs commenced around July 10. It was a pathetic sight to see the welders, fitters, and others working in the hot sun. The heat was almost unbearable to live in, let alone do manual work in the sweltering air.

I left the ship each day at around 1600 hours, mainly due to the prevailing conditions. I hailed a taxi and went to a mall about three km from the port. I sat in the mall in air-conditioned comfort and returned to the ship at around 2200 hours. During my visits to the mall, I did some shopping for I was now a man set to go home on leave.

The MD left Ras al-Khaimah around July 11, 2006. He informed me, prior to his departure, that there was a short delay in signing me off.

The repairs progressed. The ship's crew and the engine room staff were also busy carrying out a large load of work detailed by the MD. It was part of the company's "cost cutting" measures.

The new cook arrived onboard on July 15, and immediately took charge. The problem of food was resolved. It brought me a great sense of relief. Feeding the crew was not an easy task, especially without a cook.

As far as the repairs were concerned, from the way in which repairs to the ship's air-conditioning system were being carried-out, I had my reservations about the repair team. I decided to talk to the boss of that company. The boss, an engineer, met with me on July 16. The discussion was not a very pleasant one. "Mr. Yusuf, I find that your workers do not come to work daily. Once they were missing for two days. Their excuse was that you sent them to attend to another job," I said.

"Yes, captain, I did send them to attend to other work. The reason being, your boss has not yet approved my quotation. He just keeps telling us to do the job. This is not right. However, we have dismantled the broken-down compressor – it is as old as the ship. I have quoted the price to replace this with a new one, but your MD wanted me to get a reconditioned compressor. I cannot give a guarantee for a reconditioned compressor. But he keeps insisting for a guarantee," he said.

I asked him for his quotation and he immediately handed it over to me. Yes, there was a lot of work involved. But from the quotation, I found him to be a gold digger.

"I will ask the chief engineer to make a counteroffer," I said, and assured him that if he did a good job – I would watch the performance of the system for three days – that I would approve his payment directly to the agents.

I called in the chief engineer who came and studied the quotation and made a counteroffer. After pondering for a while, the boss agreed to the counteroffer. Full force work commenced the following day and the ship's air-conditioning system was restored in two days after forty-eight hours of continuous work.

I was advised by the MD, in the meantime, that it was difficult to find another captain to relieve me. He advised me to hand over temporary command of the ship to the chief officer and proceed on leave. I was advised to leave on July 24. When the chief officer was informed of the decision taken by the MD, he immediately asked me to stay on for a few more days to help him. I agreed to stay on for two more days, and to leave on July 26.

God's plan is totally foolproof. We never realize that everything happens for a reason.

As the MD's instructions were verbal, I requested that he send me an e-mail with his instructions. I received the email on the following day. In the meantime, three days had passed since completion of repairs to the ship's air conditioning system. It was working satisfactorily. I thanked God. Now my crew, after a hard day's work, would be able to have a peaceful sleep.

On July 22, I called the agent and handed over a letter requesting them to settle the bill for repairs and include the same in the ship's accounts. The telephone call from the MD came like a flash of lightning. "John, how is it that you have changed the work order and approved the bill of Mr. Yusuf?" he bellowed.

"Yes, I made that decision after pondering the situation onboard. I was not prepared to allow my crew to suffer any more because of your selfish and deplorable work ethics," I said. "What is your problem, you are leaving soon anyway?" he asked aloud. "I will be leaving. But there are another twenty-two poor souls remaining onboard. They have suffered enough – that is enough, Mr. MD," I said.

I also went on to say that it was the chief engineer who advised me on the counteroffer to the quotation, and that I thought that there was nothing wrong in it. "Okay, please don't make any changes to quotations of other workshops," he said. I assured him that I would not touch any other matters.

My officers and ratings gave me a farewell on the eve of July 25. I woke around 0500 hours on July 26, and got ready to leave. I expected the agent to board around 0700 hours. He did not come, but called and gave me bad news. The immigration officer in Ras al-Khaimah had refused to sign me off the ship without another captain to take over the command. This was as bad as it could get.

I prayed and had a strong feeling that I would be homeward bound, anyway.

I called the chief officer and gave him the news. Not knowing exactly what was going on, I wandered around on the ship.

At around 1100 hours, the agent called and said that he was with the immigration officer and wanted me to speak with him. The moment I said, "Hello" the man at the other end hollered at me. I looked into the telephone in surprise as he yelled out his final, "You cannot go!"

I called the MD, who had already arrived in Colombo by then. I asked him to help me by talking to the Sri Lankan immigration officer there and was known to him. He did not appear to be of any help. I called home and told my wife, "It seems that I have to wait until I am properly relieved. The local immigration is not allowing me to leave. What can we do, for all is in God's hands?"

I had a late lunch and was lying on my bed when I received a call from the agent at around 1530 hours. "Captain, are you ready to leave?" he asked me. "I have been ready since 0600 hours," I said. "Okay, I met with the boss of local immigration and on his suggestion, I submitted a guarantee which was my work permit. With that, he gave me written instructions to sign you off and allow you to leave Ras al-Khaimah and the UAE from the Dubai airport," he said, breaking the best piece of news for my entire voyage.

The agent was an Indian national working in Dubai on a work permit. He also said that he would be arriving onboard in about an hour, and that I ought to be ready to leave immediately.

I thanked God. I was going home. I was going to have peace and experience serenity after a very long time without it. I had dreamed of this.

The agent came onboard at around 1645 hours on July 26, 2006 and I left *Eastern Sun*. All my officers and ratings were there to see me off. Thereafter, it was about a one hour and twenty-minute drive to Dubai from Ras al-Khaimah. I truly enjoyed the drive.

I called home and my daughter came on the line. She said, "Hi, where are you?" "I am on my way to Dubai. I will be boarding the plane at Dubai airport." I replied. Then I asked her, "What do you want from Dubai? There was a short pause. "Come home, just come home." That was what she said. Then I spoke with my wife and she noted the flight number and arrival time at Colombo, and said, "We will meet you on arrival."

"Captain, your flight is at 2330 hours. Do you want to do any shopping?" asked the agent, while driving. "Yes, depending on the time I have," I said.

"My boss is waiting to meet you at the office. So I will take you there, first," he said. I agreed. Why not? They had done so much for me. A courtesy call was appropriate. "Yes," I said.

On arriving at the agent's office, I met with the young MD who was also an Indian national. I thanked him and his staff profusely for the help that they had extended to me. Thereafter, over a cup of tea, I had a discussion with him and his senior managers. The meeting lasted for about an hour. The topics were the ongoing repairs onboard, the future business of the ship, and the integrity of the owners. The agents were already settling heavy bills. I advised them to call for payments from time to time, thereby avoiding the accumulation of a huge amount to be settled at the end. They appreciated my advice.

Soon after finishing the meeting, I was taken to the shopping areas where electronic items were available for sale. I bought a karaoke set and a few other gadgets. I did not have a significant amount of money when I left the ship. It was impossible to shop until I dropped.

There was one more hurdle –immigration at the airport. Although I was off the ship, my mind was not at peace. The immigration clearance at the airport was a nagging worry. It was for this very reason that I asked the agent to take me to the airport early. He followed my advice and drove straight to the airport. I checked in and the immigration and other formalities were soon completed. I indicated to the agent, who was still there, that I was through and thanked him.

Chapter Fifteen
No Place Like Home

Now I was sure that I was homeward bound. I did some shopping at the duty-free shops in the airport. I was scheduled to fly home on SriLankan Airlines. The time was around 2100 hours, and I knew I had more than two hours to wait to board the flight. I decided to have a hearty dinner and a few undisturbed hours of sleep on the aircraft.

Basking in the glory of these thoughts, I walked into a well-appointed restaurant in the airport. I took a seat in front of a TV. The attending waiter did not waste any time and immediately came around to take the order. I ordered a glass of beer to start. Thereafter, I ordered my dinner – a fish-based meal. I was into my second beer at the time the dinner was served.

I was just digging into my dinner when I heard an announcement on the public address system. "All passengers for Colombo, please board the aircraft through the gate. I began to panic and immediately stopped eating and called the waiter. He, through his experience at working at the airport, realized that this was an emergency. He brought my check; I settled it with my credit card, and rushed to the designated gate. When I got there, I found a notice to indicate that the gate had been changed and that the flight was delayed by two hours.

It seemed like my agonies were still draining out in bits and pieces.

I could not spend money for another meal. I was starving, and also annoyed about this situation. Yet, there was nothing I could do about it. I took a seat near the newly-assigned gate and waited for the call to board the aircraft. While I was seated there, two women arrived and sat close to me. I immediately figured-out that they were Sri Lankan because they spoke the native language Sinhala. They were having a very serious discussion, and were weighing pros and cons of their employers: the harassment, the shortcomings and shortfalls in payments they had endured during the two-year period of employment in Sharjah, UAE. It was very sad to hear their stories.

As the conversation played in the back of my mind, I had a picture of my own dark experiences during the command of my ship. However, like me, they were also finally homeward bound.

One of them suddenly turned towards me and asked, "Are you from Sri Lanka?" I chuckled, because she asked the question in Sinhalese.

Sinhala is not an International language like English. "Yes, I am from Sri Lanka," I replied lightheartedly. The next question was whether I was also going back home after working in the UAE. I said, "No, I just signed off from a ship and I am now going home," I said.

"Sir, I have a son who has studied up to Advanced Level. He is now at home. He has nothing to do," said one of them. "He is not doing any work or higher studies. I am worried about him because he is an active member of a leftist political party. Sir, I am the breadwinner. My husband was an alcoholic and he died about two years ago. Other than the son, I have two daughters, a seventeen year old and a fifteen year old; they are still studying. Their brother is taking care of them. But it seems that part of the money I have sent home has been used by my son for his political work. This cannot go on, sir. I cannot leave those two young girls and come to work again. That is why I am asking you for a favor. Can you find him a job on a ship?" she pleaded.

Having listened to her story sympathetically, I asked her," How old is your son?" "My son is now twenty-one," she said. Thereafter, I explained to her that there was a time when people just simply boarded ships, especially Greek ships, when the ships berthed at the port of Colombo. These hopefuls merely showed their passports and, in many instances, had been lucky to get a job. "That system has now been done away with. To join a ship as a deck trainee, one must follow a course.

There are two colleges in Sri Lanka where these courses are conducted. You will have to pay about USD 1,000 to USD 1,500 for the entire course. On successful completion, this boy will have to find a job," I enlightened her

I saw how despair engulfed her immediately like a dark cloud. After deep thought, she continued, "Sir, this is my friend. She and I worked at two houses situated in close proximity. We were paid USD 250 for a month. I sent my entire salary home for almost eighteen months. Thereafter, I sent only USD 175 and held on to the balance to buy some jewelry for my daughters and for my shopping. Believe me, Sir, now I am going home with only USD 220 in my purse. So I hope you understand my position," she said.

Then I realized that if the boy wanted to join as a galley boy for a start, there was a way! He had to work in the kitchen of a reputed hotel or restaurant for at least six months. If he obtained a good certificate from that place, then he had only to follow some short courses such as lifesaving, firefighting, etc., and then he would be eligible to apply to the Department of Merchant Shipping for a Seaman's Book. Once he had that to show proof he had the proper training and a valid passport, he could look around for a job. I could help him, I explained to the woman. She asked for my telephone number, and I gave her my name and home telephone number.

I was distressed to learn that this woman's earnings had ceased the moment she left employment. She was going home with only USD 220. She said that she was from a village on the south part of the island. The distance from the airport to her village was around 110 miles. She would have to spend at least USD 70 to 80 for a van to go home with her baggage. What would she have in hand, finally?

Having pondered this woman's situation, I asked her, "It seems to me that you have hardly any money to survive with your family for two months. How are you going to manage? What have you planned?" I asked her in concern.

My query put her in deep thought. After a sigh, she said, "Sir, my younger daughter and I will work on a tea plantation for a daily wage. My younger daughter will not be able to do a full-time job but she will work for a few hours in the afternoon."

There were about thirty minutes left until the departure gates opened. "In case I have some news for your son, how should I contact you?" I asked her. "Sir, my brother works for the Urban Council. He is a driver and is always out of the office. If you please, call this number and ask for Martin. If he is not around, please leave a message along with your number. He will certainly call you. Just give him your name and ask him to pass the message to me. He lives in the neighborhood. By the time he comes home from work it is always around 7.00 p.m. But I will get the message. I will go to the town the first thing in the morning and call you. Sir, I hope and pray that you could help my son," she said. She handed me a piece of paper with the necessary information on it.

Thereafter, I responded to the public address system by joining the queue. They followed me and joined the queue to enter the departure gate. I lost sight of them after boarding the aircraft. But every word the woman had said echoed in my mind. I had already decided to help her son. But there was one question. If this young man was a member of a revolutionary-type political party, how would he adapt to working onboard a ship? Later, I decided that God would take care of that part.

When I had first sat in the waiting area, I was hungry and tired. But now my mind was active - diverted from hunger and fatigue after listening to the woman whose name was Catherine. I decided I would contact a friend of mine who is a philanthropist. He had helped many poor people in life-changing ways which included providing funds to undergo heart by-pass surgery and kidney transplants. He owned three tourist hotels, a few ocean-going tugs, and a small ship.

These were the thoughts that filled my mind when the plane landed at Colombo airport. I rushed to clear immigration formalities. After making a few quick purchases at the duty-free shop, I collected my baggage and left via the Green Channel with nothing to declare.

My wife and son were in the waiting area and it was good to see them. Both of them came and hugged me. My son took over the job of pushing my trolley, and none of us spoke for a while. Then I asked where my little girl was. My wife said that she had a class. She hadn't wanted to go, but was persuaded that I would be home by 11.00 a.m. and she had plenty of time to finish it and then see me.

My son turned towards me, and said, "You came home at a good time. We are into our summer holidays."

When I got into the vehicle, my wife asked me, "How are you feeling?" I said, "As if I am on top of the world!" She looked straight into my eyes and said. "I am asking about your health. You don't look good. You are sunburnt. Your eyes are sunken. All in all, to my eyes, you look very unhealthy. I can just imagine the pressure and the stress you have been under. You need to take it easy."

As a normal practice, on the way home from the airport and if it is during daytime hours, I first visit a church. This is to thank God for helping me in all the difficult times, and for bringing me home safely. In this case, I visited the Church of Our Lady of the Miraculous Medal. It was one of my favorite churches. I felt so relaxed! Finally, I was back home, my home sweet home.

We arrived at the house around 10:30 a.m. My first thought when entering the driveway was, "It's good to be home, Oh Lord. Thank you." The main door to the house was opened. As I was entering, my daughter, who had been hiding, jumped and held onto me. She hugged me and whispered, "I missed you. What has happened to you? You don't look very good! Why did you have to go through all that suffering?" I did not say anything. I just listened to her.

My wife had invited all our relations to dinner. That evening, there was quite a crowd at the house. The entertainment was the karaoke set that I bought in Dubai. It had over 2000 songs including some of my favorites: Send Me The Pillow, Massachusetts, Green Green Grass Of Home, Blue Eyes Crying In The Rain, Before The Next Teardrop Falls, Adios Amigo, Galway Bay, etc.

While the sing-song was going on, I went and sat next to my mother. Her younger sister, my Godmother, died while I was away. She looked at me, nodded her head with a questionable look on her face, and asked, "How was the ship, and how was everything?" "Well, everything was good," was my brief answer. "But to me, you have changed in your appearance. You need to take a lot of rest. When you have settled down, you should consult your physician without delay. To my eyes, you look like someone who has not had proper sleep for months." She gave me a full description of what had happened with her sister. It was very sad. Finally, she told me, "You just missed the feast of our church. Come and pay a visit to the church.

With my family, within a few hours, I started to see the change in myself – I was happy and content.

Chapter Sixteen

Dreams Come True

Finally, my mind took me on a short tour.

Ask anyone coming home from another land about the feelings that sway one's very being on landing at the airport of their motherland. For me, this feeling quadrupled before my very eyes. Not only had I been away from all things familiar for a considerable period of time, but I had had to endure the most trying of situations and conditions.

I had dreamed of being home a hundred times – they were dreams that kept me alive in the suffocating heat, in the mysterious rustle of a million cockroaches.

I could not find the words to explain all the feelings I had. All the feelings that a human being was capable of were simmering within me. From happiness to sorrow, from relief to regret, from expectation to hope, I was being drowned in a sea of human emotion.

There are no bad experiences in life, there are only lessons. And I had learned more than one lesson. I had a Master Mariner certificate, which is the highest sea-going qualification. Each of my experiences had made me stronger, more of a man and a seafarer who knew all weathers and all storms.

Today, as I look back, I think of all my experiences in troubled waters. My survival of them all has taught me of my many possibilities. Good things are never realized until they are lost. There were no good things lost on my troubled voyage. I would be failing if I did not mention the wealth of human relations and emotions that seared my very being during my long and turbulent voyage.

I had seen them all – human emotions as destructive anger, stark misery, deep want, helplessness, and suffering. Of all these emotions that reigned onboard, I could look back at the powerful and positive human emotions that changed Reema's life. Love, they say, is a very powerful emotion and it was love that got Reema back onto the right track and changed her poverty to hope and happiness.

The power of love is immense and I was so glad that love was the reigning emotion in my very being. I have always acted with love and compassion – towards the members of my crew, towards strangers, towards my family, towards my wife and children, – in short, towards everyone who needed it. This love I feel is but a magnetism sent to me from God and it is the power of His love that is reflected in my being – hence the need to help and to reach out to others.

Life is complex. It holds a sea of different situations for each of us. I have successfully battled all the storms that raged in my life. And as I now wade in my beloved land with my loved ones – those days in troubled waters seem to sink deeper into the past.

However, this is a past I will never forget.

Happy stories generally have happy endings. Sad stories are unlikely to have happy endings due to the depths of despair that sadness is capable of causing us to sink into. Sailing out of these troubled waters and putting my arms around my loved ones was perhaps the happiest ending of all.

Acknowledgements

In life, I have found there is one person who is with you all the time and that is God. I thank and praise Him for all he is doing and has done for me. In relation to this book, for forgiving me for my failures and suffering caused by following my own understanding, and not adhering to His loving word. God's mercy certainly saved me, my ship, and crew from all the adversities we faced.

My deep and sincere gratitude to my family for their strength, support, and willingness to sacrifice everything for me to proceed with a successful book project.

A very sincere thanks to my wonderful parents for being the guiding light and for giving me all the support to be where I am today. My father has now gone to his eternal rest; may his soul rest in peace.

To the person who showed me the way and guided me to the field of literature, late Rev Fr. Marceline Jayakody, my English teacher at St. Joseph's College: I offer my humble thanks to you, Reverend, sir.

It is not easy to get to the top of any professional qualification, including the highest sea-going qualification of Master Mariner. I would like to express my sincere thanks to my teachers in my professional studies: Mr. Gerard Trant, Capt. John Archer, Capt. T.K. Joseph, late Capt. S.S.S. Rewari, late Capt. H. Subramaniam, and Capt. Evan Williams for educating and guiding me to pass the exam of Master Mariner and have the privilege of commanding ships.

Meeting Alinka Rutkowska was not a coincidence. I consider it to be a God-given opportunity. I thank Alinka and her wonderful team at Leaders Press for undertaking this book project with the hopes of taking my story to all corners of the world.

Last but not least, to you, my sincere reader: without you, I am nothing. I thank every reader for selecting and reading my book.

About the Author

John De Silva was born in the post-independent era of Ceylon (as Sri Lanka was well known then) and now lives in Maryland, USA, with his family.

He had his secondary education at a leading Catholic school in Colombo, where he came under the tutelage and influence of the late Rev. Father Marceline Jayakody, a versatile writer and a national literary figure. He had his baptism in writing under the watchful eyes of Rev. Father Jayakody.

But a chance meeting with an officer in the merchant Navy along with a visit to a ship berthed in the Colombo harbor developed a youthful fascination for seafaring in him.

John De Silva joined the merchant Navy as an Officer Cadet in 1973. After fourteen years of sailing, and having done intermediate studies at Sir John Cass College in London and at Lal Bahadur Shastri Nautical & Engineering College in Mumbai, he joined the Sydney Maritime College and graduated as a Master Mariner in 1989. Since then, he has been commanding merchant ships around the globe. He is also a marine surveyor and a consultant.

After having sailed for about thirty years—out of which he had been in command of various ships for about twelve—Captain John De Silva began the odyssey depicted in *Captain's Logbook*.

John De Silva continued to sail until he decided to say goodbye to sea life in 2015. Thereafter, he continued with his writing, and he was the scriptwriter and producer of a teleseries in Sri Lanka that consisted of 84 episodes and won eight awards. He now works as a Marine Surveyor.